The Australian Women's Weekly craft library

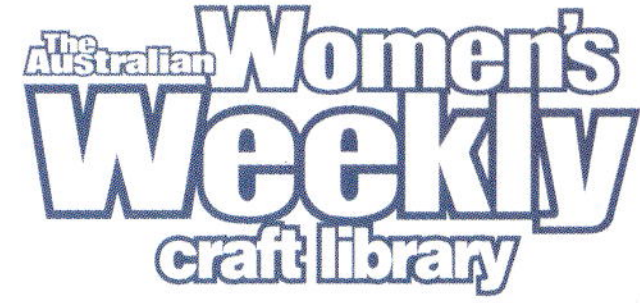

BABY gifts

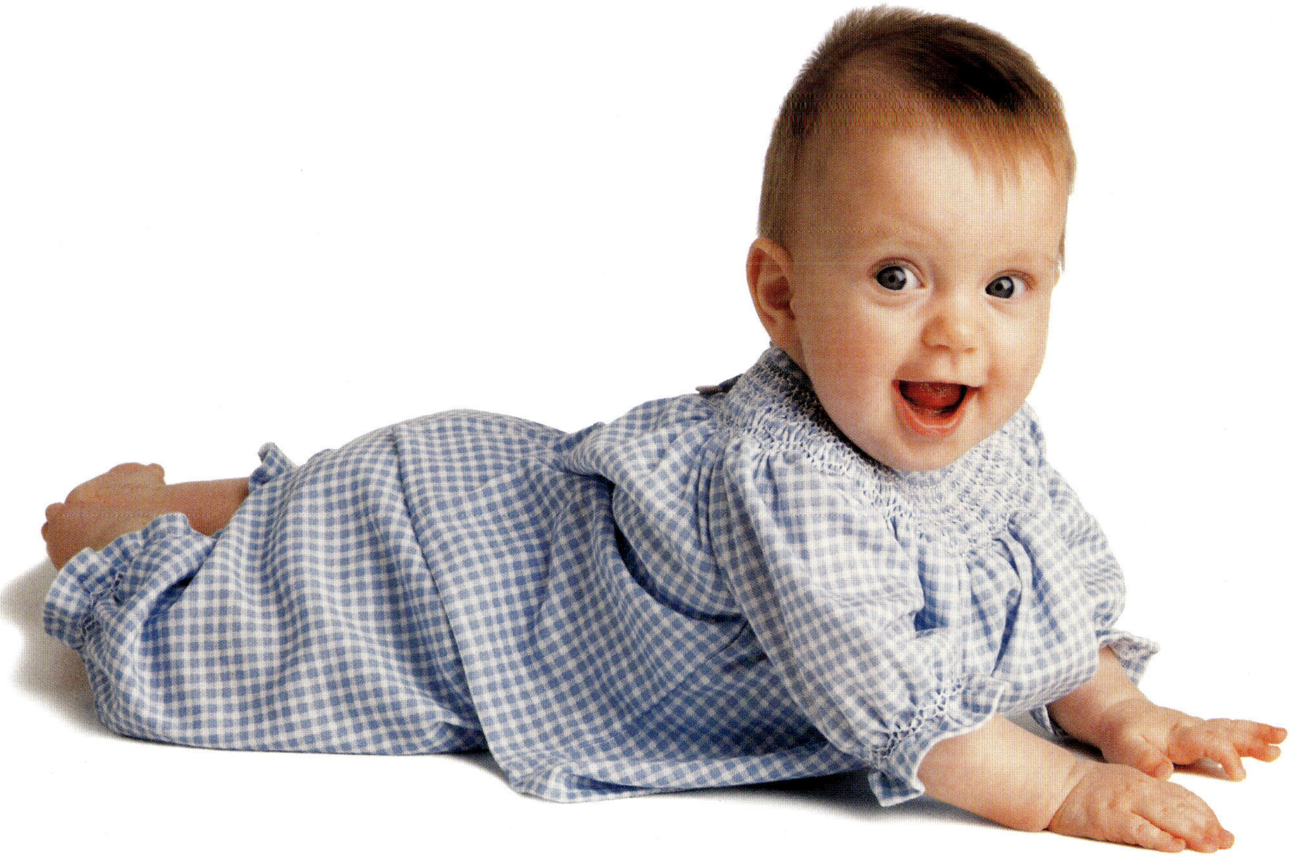

contents

Rebecca
Sara Fraser
Gribble
November
21st 1999

small THINGS BRIGHT and BEAUTIFUL

Decorating a nursery can be great fun, and never more so than with this delightful naïve appliqué. Brightly coloured animals, birds and abstract shapes create a veritable kaleidoscope of cheerful images that will delight both baby and you. Using two different colourways, to show how you can adapt the ideas to a colour scheme of your choice, we've used the simple little shapes on lots of nursery paraphernalia – from quilts, curtains and wall-hangings to clothing, lampshades, mobiles and soft toys.

OPPOSITE: Sunlight filtering through a pair of appliquéd curtains makes the nursery glow with colour. Using inexpensive white cotton, appliqué shapes cut from a variety of colourful coordinating scraps and occasional touches of hand embroidery, the curtains were created for next to nothing. A solid border and matching tags make hanging very easy – but if you don't want to go to this extra trouble, simply appliqué onto readymade plain curtains. Appliqué instructions are on page 118.

OPPOSITE: Tiny babies will respond to the bright colours of this nursery wall-hanging and, as they grow, will adore learning and reciting the names of the various animals and shapes. Gather a collection of coordinating fabric scraps in the colours of your choice and have fun adding all the amusing little extra bits and pieces. If a wall-hanging seems like too much work, try making a cushion instead. Or stitch up a very easy lovable soft toy, simply using an enlarged appliqué outline (see instructions on page 11).

Wall-Hanging

Measurements

Finished size is approximately 70cm square.

Materials

- 1.5m x 112cm plain background fabric
- 0.3m x 90cm print fabric, for border
- Scraps of various prints and plains for appliqué and tabs
- Double-sided appliqué paper, such as Vliesofix
- Pencil
- Sharp scissors
- Matching and contrast machine thread
- Stranded embroidery cotton in matching and contrast shades
- Buttons, bows and pompoms, for embellishment
- Stick or dowel pole, for hanging
- Acrylic paint, in desired colours
- Gloss varnish

Method

1 BACKGROUND Cut two 74cm squares of background fabric (measurement includes 1.5cm seam allowances) and set one aside for backing.

2 BORDER From border print, cut four 62cm x 7cm strips. Place the strips on your work surface in a rough square, right side up, so that you can see which way the mitred corners should go. Fold one corner at the end of each strip at a 45 degree angle, finger press and cut along fold line to form mitre angles. With right sides together, stitch angled edges of borders together, starting and stopping stitching 1cm from inner and outer edge of each seam. Press seams open, trim excess fabric at corners and press under 1cm on each inner and outer edge of border. You should now have a frame-like border with neatly mitred corners.

Position border frame on background fabric so that it is equidistant from each edge and baste in place close to each pressed edge.

3 APPLIQUÉ Using the methods described under **Basic Appliqué Techniques**, on page 118, appliqué 25 designs of your choice within the border, in five rows of five, using the photograph as a guide and alternating a cut-out square with an animal. Decorate each animal with extra embellishment, such as a pompom tail, ribbon bow, button or tassel, but do not finish with decorative embroidery at this stage.

4 HANGING LOOPS From different fabrics, make five hanging loops, each 4cm wide (finished width). The length of the loops will depend on the thickness of your hanging rod, but don't forget to add seam allowance on each end. With right sides together and raw edges even, position and baste both raw ends of each loop to the top edge of the hanging, at evenly-spaced intervals.

5 BACKING With right sides together, stitch backing fabric to front, sandwiching loops at the same time and leaving an opening in one side for turning. Turn right side out, slipstitch opening closed and press. Starting at the centre and working towards the edges, baste the layers together with several lines of stitching, keeping layers smooth and wrinkle-free as you work. Topstitch inner edge of basted border, close to pressed edge, then do the same for the outer edge.

6 EMBROIDERY Using three strands of contrast embroidery thread, work a row of decorative stitches (see **Embroidery Stitch Guide** on page 112) around outer edge of border, using the photograph as a guide, and working through all layers of fabric. Work outer embroidered borders and decorative stitching around appliqué in the same way, working through all layers so that backing can't "balloon" or sag. Remove basting.

7 FINISHING Decorate stick or rod, as desired, with paint and a coat of varnish. When dry, insert into loops for hanging.

Creating a colour coordinated nursery doesn't have to be an expensive affair, and appliqué is one of the easiest and cheapest ways of unifying various bits and pieces, since it uses so little fabric. Here, a readymade bath sheet and face washer have been turned into a matching gift set, while the very necessary but rather ordinary foam rubber change pad has been covered with soft and absorbent white towelling then jazzed up with colourful appliquéd animals. Since change pads come in different sizes, you will need to make your own pattern. If the pad comes with its own cover, you can unpick this and use the pieces for a pattern. Otherwise, make a template of the end shape by standing the pad on its end and tracing around the outline (don't forget to add seam allowance to your traced line). Next, measure around the complete width, from centre back to centre back (plus seam allowance) and make a rectangular paper pattern to this measurement x the length of the pad, from end to end (plus seams). Ascertain on your pattern where the sides will fall and fingerpress the fabric to mark fold lines. Appliqué between the fold lines, as desired. The shaped ends could also be decorated if you choose. Insert a zip in the centre back seam, then stitch the end sections in place. You could also appliqué onto a plain readymade cover, if you prefer.

Toddlers just love checking how much they've grown and this is a clever way to plot their progress. Simple to make, the growth chart is a charming nursery decoration, aside from its practical purpose, and would make a lovely gift for a first birthday. When hanging it, you will need to check that the lowest measurement is exactly 50cm from the floor. By using a fine fabric marker to plot and date the child's growth, you will then have a permanent record to keep for posterity, and no problems with pencil marks on the architrave when the room finally needs re-decorating!

Growth Chart

Measurements

Finished chart is 20cm x 87cm.

Materials

- 0.5m x 112cm plain background fabric
- Scraps of different prints, for appliqué
- 0.25m x 112cm iron-on interfacing
- Double-sided appliqué webbing, such as Vliesofix
- Matching and contrasting machine thread
- Contrast stranded embroidery cottons
- Two x 26cm lengths 15mm-diameter dowel, for hanging
- Acrylic paint
- Cord, for hanging

Method

1 BACKGROUND From background fabric, cut two rectangles, each 23cm x 100cm (includes 1.5cm seam allowance). Fold one rectangle in half crosswise and fingerpress to mark centre point. Using light pencil marks and a ruler, measure seven 5cm increments above and below this centre point. Don't forget to allow for the 1.5cm seam allowance on the side when marking your lines. Lightly pencil in figures at 10cm intervals – and don't worry if your writing looks a little rustic; that only adds to the charm.

2 APPLIQUÉ & EMBROIDERY Following the **Basic Appliqué Techniques**, on page 118, and using the photograph as a guide, appliqué six evenly spaced designs on the lefthand side of the front. Choose the motifs that please you, not necessarily those in the picture. Finish appliqué with embroidery and work measurement marks and figures in stem stitch (see **Embroidery Stitch Guide** on page 112), taking the stitching a little way into the seam allowance so that marks will start right on the edge on the finished chart.

3 BACKING Cut a piece of interfacing, 23cm x 100cm, and apply to the wrong side of appliquéd front. Cut off corners of interfacing only, to make seams less bulky.

With right sides together, stitch front to back, leaving an opening for turning in one side. Turn right side out, slipstitch opening closed and press.

4 FINISHING Turn under 5cm on each short edge and stitch close to the edge to secure, forming casing. Paint dowel lengths in the colour of your choice and thread through casings at top and bottom. Attach a cord to each end of the top rod, for hanging.

From the appliqué shapes on the pattern sheet, we chose the horse to enlarge into a soft toy, but several of the other outlines would also be suitable, and if you don't want to make separate legs, simply cut them as part of a single pattern piece, making the sewing very easy indeed.

Soft Toy

Measurements

Finished toy stands approximately 20cm high. We give a pattern for the horse, but you could use any of the shapes. If you choose a different one, enlarge your chosen outline to 200%.

Materials

- 0.2m x 90cm print fabric
- Polyester fibrefill
- Stranded embroidery cotton in several colours
- Four x 1.5cm-diameter buttons

Pattern pieces

Pattern pieces are printed on pattern sheet in a pink tone. Trace Horse Body, Ear and Leg.

Cutting

NOTE 5mm seam allowance is included on all pieces, unless otherwise indicated.

From print fabric, cut two Bodies, four Ears and eight Legs.

Method

Unless otherwise indicated, all seams are stitched with right sides together.

1 EARS Stitch Ears together in pairs, leaving lower edge open. Clip corners and turn right side out. Fill very lightly with a little polyester fibrefill and baste raw edges together. With raw edges even, baste Ears in position on one Body section.

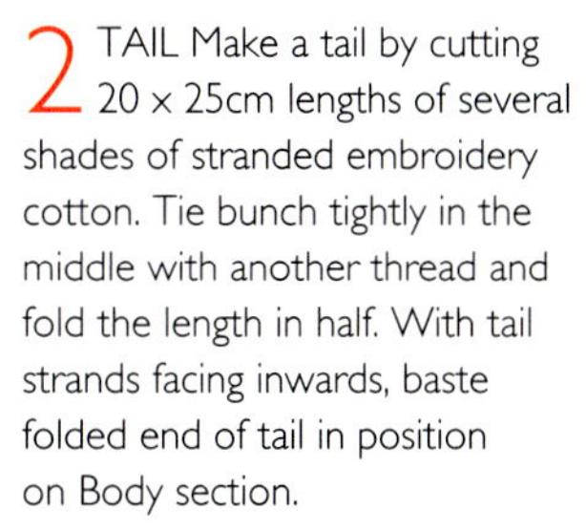

2 TAIL Make a tail by cutting 20 x 25cm lengths of several shades of stranded embroidery cotton. Tie bunch tightly in the middle with another thread and fold the length in half. With tail strands facing inwards, baste folded end of tail in position on Body section.

3 BODY Stitch Bodies together, sandwiching tail and Ears at the same time and leaving an opening for turning in lower edge. Clip curves, turn right side out, fill with fibrefill and slipstitch opening closed.

4 LEGS Stitch Legs together in pairs, leaving an opening in one side for turning. Clip corners and turn right side out. Fill each Leg with fibrefill and slipstitch opening closed. Stitch Legs to each side of Body, using a small button on each side as a washer, so that Legs can be moved. Make sure that Legs are attached very firmly and that thread is securely tied off.

5 FINISHING Using the photograph as a guide, stitch eye and other details with embroidery thread, and trim tail.

The appliqué designs of the previous pages assume an entirely new look in a different colourway, as you can see here. It's the small details that make a difference in any decorating scheme and here are two such charming little details – a lampshade appliquéd and stitched to match the rest of the nursery décor, and a simple appliquéd picture to delight a small child.

Lampshade

Measurements

Method can be adapted to any purchased shade.

Materials

- Purchased white lampshade
- Background fabric
- Contrast fabric for bias trim
- Scraps of different appliqué fabrics
- Double-sided appliqué webbing
- Machine thread
- Stranded embroidery cotton
- Craft glue

Method

1 BACKGROUND Make a paper template from your lampshade by rolling it along a large sheet of paper, marking the top and bottom outlines as you roll. Cut this piece from background fabric, on the bias, adding 1.5cm seam allowance at each end for centre seam.

2 APPLIQUÉ Following the **Basic Appliqué Techniques** on page 118, and using the photograph as a guide, appliqué four or five evenly-spaced designs around the shade fabric. Finish with embroidered detail in contrast colours.

3 CONSTRUCTING SHADE With right sides together, pin centre seam of shade and place it onto the purchased shade for a test fit. It should fit snugly. Adjust, if necessary, and stitch, then press seam open.

4 BINDING From contrast fabric, cut and join enough 4cm-wide bias strips to fit around both top and bottom edges of shade, plus turnings. Press under 5mm on each long edge of both top and bottom bindings, then press in half lengthwise, wrong sides together.

Open out one long edge of top binding and, starting at centre back seam, with right sides together, baste binding to top edge of shade, placing raw edge of binding 1cm below raw edge of shade. Stitch as basted, folding in raw ends. Turn binding to inside and slipstitch in place. Finish binding seam with contrast embroidered stitches, as photographed.

Open out one long edge of remaining binding strip and stitch to lower edge of shade, as for upper edge. Do not fold remaining edge of binding to inside. Work decorative embroidery over seam, as before.

5 FINISHING Place shade onto purchased lampshade, matching seams. Fold lower edge of bias around to inside and glue in place, smoothing out any wrinkles as you work.

BELOW: Babies are fascinated by the colour and movement of mobiles and this one is sure to provide many hours of soothing contemplation. From the appliqué motifs on the pattern sheet, choose the shapes that you prefer and cut their outlines from felt (two sides for each). There's no need to add seam allowance – simply blanket stitch the shapes together with embroidery cotton (see **Embroidery Stitch Guide**, on page 112), fill lightly and add features with embroidery thread or by gluing contrast felt pieces in place. Using fine cord or wool, string the shapes from two brightly painted child-size coathangers that have been screwed together at right angles by the hook. Cover or paint hook and hang mobile above the cot, well out of baby's reach. The same felt shapes could also be strung across a basinette to divert a tiny occupant.

OPPOSITE: A standard white cot is transformed with a delicately sheer canopy, appliquéd in various blues and greens and highlighted with a gingham border and rows of hand-embroidered stitching. Small shapes have been cut from the same outlines (don't forget to add seam allowance), and stitched together for matching cot trinkets. Enlarge the outlines on a photocopier if you'd prefer bigger toys. Finish with metal eyelets and hang from contrasting ribbons. The wall-hanging, on page 7, has been converted here into a pretty cot quilt. If making a quilt, you will need to topstitch through all layers around the gingham borders and outline-quilt some of the motifs in order to hold the top, batting and backing securely together. You could also use embroidery thread to "tie" the layers together, if desired.

OPPOSITE: This colourful hanging bag provides the perfect storage place for those indispensable items in every nursery – nappies. Hung above the change table or behind a door, the stacker will keep a pile of cloth or disposable nappies clean, out of sight and, most importantly, close at hand for that inevitable next change.

Nappy Stacker

Measurements

Finished stacker is 68cm long (excluding hook) x 35cm wide.

Materials

- 0.6m x 115cm green fabric
- 0.4m x 115cm blue fabric
- Scraps of blue and green checks and prints, for appliqué
- Double-sided appliqué webbing, such as Vliesofix
- Matching machine threads
- Stranded embroidery cottons
- Firm cardboard rectangle, 19.5cm x 33.5cm
- Baby-sized wooden coathanger, with metal hook (see NOTE, below)

NOTE The pattern is designed to fit a baby-sized coathanger, 31cm long. These are usually available in craft stores, but if you can't find one, cut the ends from an adult-sized hanger and sand the raw edges smooth.

Pattern piece

Pattern piece is printed on the pattern sheet in a pink tone. Trace Nappy Stacker Top. The remainder of the pieces are squares and rectangles (see below).

Cutting

NOTE 1cm seam allowance is **included** on pattern piece and given measurements, unless otherwise indicated.

From green fabric, cut two 56cm squares for the Side sections, and three rectangles, each 37cm x 23cm, for the Base.

From blue fabric, cut two Tops, and two strips, each 4cm x 56cm, for Front Binding.

Method

1 SIDE SECTIONS With right sides together, stitch Side sections together along centre back seam. Press seam open.

2 FRONT BINDING With right sides together and raw edges even, stitch a blue Binding strip to each centre front edge. Press seam towards Binding. Press under seam allowance on remaining long raw edge of Binding, fold Binding to wrong side and slipstitch pressed edge in place over seam.

3 INVERTED SIDE PLEATS With right sides together, fold each Side section in half towards the centre so that bound centre front edges align with each other along centre back seam. Measure in along top edge 10cm from each fold and mark with a pin. Rule a 6cm line downwards from each of these marker pins. Starting at the top edge, stitch along ruled lines to create pleats, backstitching at end of each line to reinforce. Press pleat flat, bringing stitching to the centre, creating an inverted pleat. Baste across upper edge of pleat, to hold.

4 APPLIQUÉ Using the photograph as a guide and following the **Basic Appliqué Techniques** on page 118, appliqué one Top section and the opening edges of the Sides, as desired. Use stranded embroidery cotton to add French knot eyes and other details, as you wish. When all appliqué is complete, press sections well.

5 BASE To reinforce lower edge of Side section, stitch along lower edge, along seam line. To mark corners for Base, starting at one centre front edge, measure in 17cm along lower edge and mark with a pin. From this pin, measure a distance of 21cm and mark with a pin. Now measure 34cm along and mark as before; measure another 21cm along and mark. The final distance back to second centre front edge should be 17cm. At each of these pin markers, which represent the corners of the Base rectangle, clip across seam allowance as far as (but not through) the reinforcing line of stitching.

With right sides together, pin one Base rectangle to lower edge of Side section, with centre front edges meeting in centre of one long edge of Base, centre back seam aligned with centre of opposite long edge of Base, and matching clipped corner markers to corners of Base, easing Side carefully around corners. Baste, then stitch as basted. Press seam towards Base. On the outside, topstitch Base, close to seam.

6 TOP With right sides together, stitch Top sections together around curved edge, leaving open between small dots at top. Clip curves, turn right side out and press.

7 JOINING TOP TO SIDE With right sides together and with centre front edges meeting at centre front of appliquéd Top section, and with seams of Top aligned with pleat stitching at sides, stitch Top to upper edge of Side section. Press seam towards Top. On outside, topstitch Top close to seam.

8 BASE INSERT With right sides together, stitch remaining Base sections together, leaving one short edge open. Trim corners, turn right side out and press. Insert firm cardboard into Base, fold in raw edges and slipstitch opening closed. Place Base Insert into stacker to reinforce Base.

9 HANGER & HOOK From a scrap of fabric, cut a bias strip, 4cm x 15cm. Fold strip in half lengthwise, right sides together, and stitch 6mm from fold. Stitch again, 7mm from fold. Cut off excess fabric close to second row of stitching. Turn bias strip right side out (using a needle and double thread to pull it through – see diagram, page 24). Tuck top raw end inside and secure with a couple of tiny stitches. Pull cover over hook and trim any excess length. Screw hook into wooden hanger and secure hook cover in place by stitching into the cover at base of hook, taking thread around hanger a couple of times, then back into hook cover. Tie off securely. Insert hanger into the Top of the stacker, bringing the hook out through the hole left in the Top.

Naturally, we couldn't resist stitching the appliqué motifs to a range of clothing, both purchased and homemade. Adding the designs to readymade babywear is an ideal way to create a delightfully personalised gift without needing to spend too much time and trouble – the range of inexpensive baby clothing that is appropriate for embellishment is almost limitless, from all-in-one suits, pilchers and singlets, to T-shirts, pinafores, caps and little jackets.

For a small project, involving only one or two motifs, you don't even need a sewing machine – simply follow the **Basic Appliqué Techniques** on page 118, but once the pieces are fused onto the background fabric, stitch around the outline by hand, using small, neat blanket stitch (see page 112 for the **Embroidery Stitch Guide**).

Of course, if you have the time to sew, you can use the motifs to combine homemade and purchased garments into a matching set, such as the practical pull-on trousers (with popper crotch opening) and purchased T-shirt, opposite, or the saucy little sailor cap on this page, that can be made to match a readymade outfit. Instructions for sewing the Trousers are on page 99 and the Sailor Cap on page 100. Patterns are sized to fit babies aged 6, 12 and 18 months.

OPPOSITE: A set of inexpensive graduated craftwood boxes has been painted with acrylic paint, then decorated with fabric, "appliqué" and buttons for a pretty and practical way to hold all the million and one small things that seem to accumulate when a baby arrives on the scene. This is a simple no-sew project that would make a delightful gift. Simply choose the designs you like from the collection on the pattern sheet (adapting them to the size of your box, if necessary). Cut them from fabric scraps that have been stiffened with iron-on interfacing or HeatNBond to prevent fraying, then glue them to the painted background. You could also cut the shapes from printed papers, if preferred. Decorate the motifs and boxes with extras, as desired. The "stitching" around the appliqué, as well as the finishing details, have all been added with dimensional paint in a contrasting colour.

Handmade gift tags and cards are a nice way to personalise a baby gift or say welcome to a new arrival. Use the photographs as a guide to create cards in your chosen colourway, using coloured cardboard, paper, fabric scraps, dimensional paint and coordinating buttons.

beach BABIES

Here's a delightful set of clothes for summer babies, featuring a cool crisp sundress with matching bloomers and sunhat, a roomy romper with coordinating shirt, and lots of mix-and-match easy cotton knits for cooler days – all sized to fit babies aged 6, 12 and 18 months.

OPPOSITE: Ashley's little sundress with cross-over straps looks sweet and fresh made up in a pretty floral print, with matching bloomers and wide-brimmed reversible hat. For cooler weather, add a knitted cotton tunic, embroidered with simple lazy daisies in colours to match the floral print.

THIS PAGE: James wears a blue cotton knitted vest over his romper and a chambray shirt, featuring collar and cuffs in a tiny blue check (see opposite bottom inset). Both vest and cute-as-a-button matching cap (plus moccasins, not shown) have contrast cross stitched bands added after knitting – giving the effect of Fair Isle with none of the headaches.

Instructions for sewing begin overleaf.
Knitting instructions begin on page 104.

Shirt

Measurements

*To fit baby aged 6 (**12**, 18) months. Finished length of Shirt is approximately 27 (**29**, 31)cm.*

Materials

- 0.6m x 115cm main fabric
- 0.2m x 90cm contrast fabric
- 0.2m x 90cm iron-on interfacing
- Seven small buttons
- Small hook and eye

Pattern pieces

Pattern pieces are printed on pattern sheet in black. Trace Front 19, Back 20, Collar 21, Neck Binding 22, Sleeve 23, Wrist Band 24 and Button Loop 25.

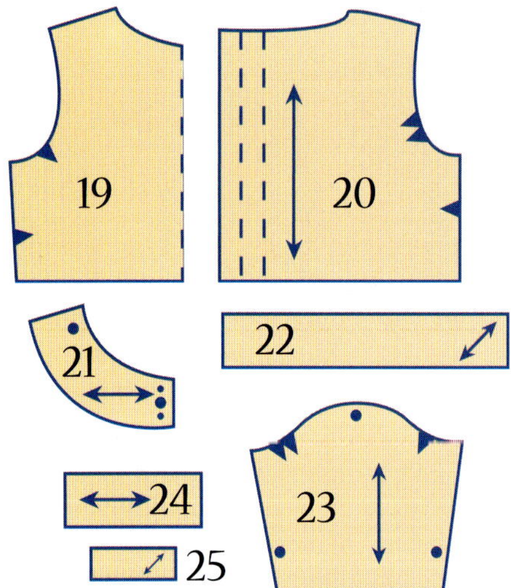

Cutting

NOTE 1.5cm seam allowance is **included** on all pattern pieces, unless otherwise indicated.

From main fabric, cut one Front, two Backs, one Neck Binding and two Sleeves.

From contrast fabric, cut four Collars, two Wrist Bands and two Button Loops.

From interfacing, cut two Collars.

Method

Unless otherwise indicated, all seams are stitched with right sides together.

1 JOINING FRONT TO BACK Stitch Front to Backs at shoulders. Trim and neaten seams.

2 SLEEVES Run an easing thread around Sleeve crown between notches. Pin Sleeves to armholes and stitch, matching shoulder dot to shoulder seam and adjusting easing where necessary to avoid puckers. Trim and neaten seam. Stitch side and Sleeve seam in one continuous operation, matching underarm seams and stopping stitching at small dot on lower edge of Sleeve to allow for opening.

3 SLEEVE OPENING Turn under and handstitch a narrow hem on each side of Sleeve opening. Run a gathering thread along wrist edge of each Sleeve. With raw edges even, pin Wrist Band to Sleeve, allowing 5mm on each end of Band to extend beyond opening edges of Sleeve. Pull up gathers to fit Band and stitch. Trim seam allowance to 5mm. Fold under 5mm on remaining long raw edge of Band, then fold Band in half to outside, right sides together. Stitch across short ends of Band, allowing 5mm seams. Trim corners, then turn Band back to inside and slipstitch pressed edge in place over seam. Topstitch around all edges of Band, if desired.

4 BUTTON LOOPS Fold bias strips in half lengthwise, right sides together, and stitch, allowing 1cm seams. Trim seam allowance. Following diagrams, below, thread a large needle with a double length of strong thread. Fasten thread at seam at one end of bias tube, then insert needle, eye first, into tube (**Diagram 1**). Work needle through tube to other end, then gradually pull tube right side out (**Diagram 2**).

Press tubing flat and fold in half, as shown, so that halfway point forms apex of triangle. Stitch across base of triangle to hold, then stitch butted sides of flattened tubing together, leaving an opening for button, as shown, on one piece (**Diagrams 3 & 4**), but stitching the other along its entire length. Press again.

5 COLLAR Press interfacing to wrong sides of two Collar pieces (Upper Collars). Position Button Loops on right side of Upper Collars, between small dots at centre front so that, when stitched, each Loop will extend 2.5cm from seam line to apex. Stitch Upper and Lower Collars together, sandwiching Loops and leaving neck edge open. Trim seam, clip curves, turn Collars right side out and press. Topstitch close to all finished edges.

6 ATTACHING COLLAR TO SHIRT Stay-stitch neck edge of Collars, then clip curves to stitching. With Under Collars facing right side of shirt, baste Collars to neck edge of shirt, matching centre fronts and backs. Press under opening edge of Backs along first fold line. Fold facing to outside along second fold line, right sides together, sandwiching Collar at neck edge. Pin bias Neck Binding strip to neck edge, right sides together and raw edges even. Stitch through all layers. Trim seam to 5mm. Turn under raw edge on Neck Binding and slipstitch in place.

7 FACING Fold facing back to inside. Open out facing at lower edge, then press up 1.5cm on lower edge. Trim seam across facing to 7mm. Fold facing to outside, along second fold line, right sides together, and stitch across lower edge, allowing 7mm seam. Fold facing back to inside, press under 7mm raw edge on hem and machine-stitch in place.

8 FINISHING Work four evenly-spaced buttonholes in left Back and sew buttons to right Back to correspond. Stitch small hook and eye (or work a thread eye) to neck edge. Stitch a button to fully stitched Button Loop, and fasten as photographed.

Diagrams for Button Loops

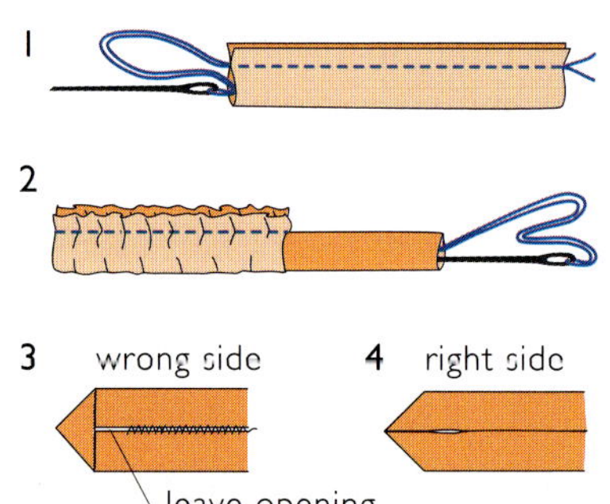

Instructions for sewing Romper, Sundress, Bloomers and Sunhat begin on page 102.

Covered Coathanger with Monogrammed Sachet

Measurements

Finished hanger is about 36cm long.

Materials

- Baby-sized wooden coathanger (see NOTE, below)
- Polyester wadding
- 0.2m x 90cm fabric
- 0.3m x 90cm contrast fabric
- 10cm square 14-count Aida cloth, for embroidery
- Stranded embroidery cotton
- Dried lavender

NOTE Baby-sized wooden coathangers (31cm) with screw-in hooks are available from craft stores. If you can't find a baby-sized hanger, cut the ends off a larger one, and sand smooth again before proceeding. The hangers can be made with purchased bias binding, if preferred. If you choose this option, you will not need contrast fabric.

Pattern piece

Pattern piece is printed on the pattern sheet in a pink tone. Trace Coathanger Section.

Cutting

NOTE 1cm seam allowance is **included** on pattern piece.

From fabric, cut four Coathanger Sections, on the bias.

From contrast fabric, cut several 3cm-wide bias strips and join to make four continuous bias strips, about 45cm each. Cut one extra 20cm x 4cm bias strip for covering hook.

Method

1 PADDING With metal hook inserted into hanger, wrap a 3-5cm-wide strip of polyester wadding around coathanger to pad it evenly. (Join several polyester strips if necessary to get required length.) Secure end of wadding in place with a couple of stitches.

2 FLAT PIPING Fold three 45cm bias strips in half lengthwise, wrong sides together, and stitch 3-4mm from fold. With right sides together and raw edges even, pin a flat piping length to two mirror-image Coathanger sections, easing piping neatly around curved ends. Stitch as pinned, following piping stitching line. Reserve remaining length of flat piping for sachet.

3 JOINING COVERS With right sides together, stitch remaining fabric Coathanger sections to piped sections, following piping stitching line. Clip curves and turn covers right side out.

4 HOOK Fold remaining bias strip in half lengthwise, right sides together and edges matching. Stitch 6-7mm from fold, then stitch again, 7-8mm from fold. Cut off excess fabric close to second row of stitching. Turn bias right side out (see page 24), then slide cover over hook. Tuck top raw end inside and hand-stitch end to secure. Pull cover firmly down over hook, trim away excess length and secure lower edge to wadding with a few firm stitches.

5 COVERING HANGER Pull covers onto each end of padded hanger, turn in raw edges at centres and slipstitch neatly together.

Scraps of leftover fabric have been used to make these pretty covered coathangers, trimmed with cross stitched lavender sachets – a delightful gift, with or without the garments to match.

6 EMBROIDERED MONOGRAM Using two strands of embroidery thread and following the alphabet graph on the pattern sheet, embroider chosen monogram onto centre of Aida square, adding extra decorative stitches in a contrast colour, if desired (see photograph). When embroidery is complete, trim corners from square to form a diamond. Cut a scrap of fabric or contrast fabric into a diamond shape to match Aida.

7 STITCHING SACHET Using reserved length of flat piping, add piped border around edge of Aida diamond, following piping stitching. With right sides together, stitch backing to Aida sandwiching piping at same time and leaving one edge open. Turn sachet right side out, fill with lavender, fold in raw edges and slipstitch opening closed.

8 ROULEAU TRIM Fold remaining 45cm bias strip in half lengthwise and, following the method for the hook cover, **Step 4**, at left, make a length of rouleau to trim hanger. Fold in half and stitch folded end to top point of sachet, then tie remaining ends around hook and finish in a bow.

Smocking and baby clothes are traditional partners and we just couldn't resist this aptly named angel suit. Made up in a checked cotton knit and designed to fit babies from birth to six months, the two-piece outfit features simple bands of smocking around the yoke and on the edges of sleeves and pants. If you've not tried smocking before, this is a great place to start.

Smocked Angel Suit

Measurements

Sized to fit babies up to 6 months.

Materials

- 0.8m x 150cm cotton knit fabric (we used blue and white check)
- Iron-on 6mm smocking dots (or a smocking pleater)
- Three small buttons
- 41cm x 12mm-wide ribbed elastic
- One skein DMC Stranded Embroidery Cotton in preferred colour

NOTE Although cotton knit is a lovely soft fabric for a baby, you could also use a fine cotton print or tiny-checked gingham.

Pattern pieces

Pattern pieces are printed on pattern sheet in pink. Trace Front 26, Back 27, Sleeve 28, Neck Binding 29 and Pants Front/Back 30.

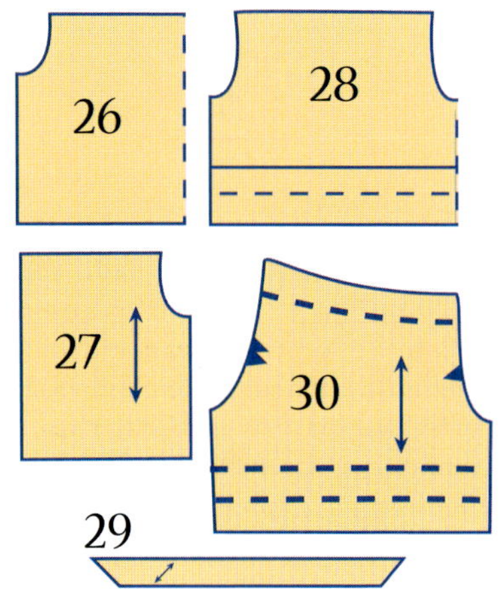

Cutting

NOTE 1cm seam allowance is **included** on all pieces unless otherwise indicated. 2.5cm casing and hem allowance are also included where appropriate. Sleeve piece is cut on the fold and cut into two pieces after pleating.

From cotton knit fabric, cut one Front, two Backs, one Sleeve (see NOTE, above), one Neck Binding (on bias) and two Pants Front/Backs.

Method

PANTS

SMOCKING PLEATS Neaten raw leg edges of Pants Front/Backs. Apply five rows of smocking dots, or pleat five half-space rows, placing first row of pleats as indicated

on pattern and, if using a gingham knit, using the lines of the checks to keep a straight line. Make sure pleating threads are long enough, as you need to keep the fabric flat to finish hem.

2 HEM Turn up and finish leg edges with a small machine hem. Pull out two pleats at either side and, with right sides together, join inside leg seams.

3 SMOCKING Using three strands of embroidery cotton and following the **Basic Smocking Stitches** and smocking graph on page 119, smock lower edges of Pants.

4 CROTCH SEAM When embroidery is complete, place one leg inside the other, right sides together, and stitch crotch seam from centre front to centre back.

5 CASING Neaten raw waist edge and turn in along fold line to form casing. Stitch close to both edges, leaving an opening for elastic. Insert elastic to fit, secure ends and close opening.

TOP

1 SLEEVE PLEATING Neaten lower raw edge of Sleeve piece. Apply five rows of smocking dots, or pleat five half-space rows, placing first row of pleats as indicated on pattern and making sure pleating threads are long enough. Cut Sleeve into two separate pieces along fold line. Undo two pleats at each side and leave threads and Sleeves flat at this point.

2 RAGLAN SEAMS Join Sleeves to Back and Front along raglan seams, using a French seam or overlocked seam, for extra neatness.

3 BACK/FRONT PLEATING & SMOCKING Apply nine rows of dots, or pleat nine half-space rows along neck edge of Top. Pull up pleats to measure 23cm around neck edge row and 41cm around bottom row, having removed 2cm of pleats from each edge of centre back. Fan out other rows evenly between neck edge row and bottom row. Work smocking, using three strands of thread and following smocking graph, on page 119. When smocking is complete, do not remove pleating threads.

4 SLEEVE & SIDE SEAMS With right sides together, stitch Sleeve and side seams in one continuous operation.

5 SLEEVES Turn up and finish hem on lower edge of Sleeves. Pull up pleating threads on Sleeves and smock as for the lower edges of Pants.

6 HEMS Neaten lower raw edge of Top, then turn under a small hem and machine-stitch or handsew in place. Turn under 5mm on centre back edges, turn under another 5mm and stitch hem in place by hand.

7 NECK BINDING With right sides together, stitch bias neck binding to neck edge, just above cable row. Turn binding to inside, fold in raw edge and slipstitch folded edge in place, turning in centre back edges at the same time.

8 FINISHING Remove all pleating threads. Sew three buttons to left centre back and work three button loops on right centre back to correspond.

snow WHITE

However much the world changes, some things remain the same and family traditions provide a comforting sense of order in a changing world. If christening a new member is an important event in your family, you'll appreciate the delightful tradition of an heirloom christening dress, worn by each new baby on its special day, then carefully folded away for babies as yet unborn.

This pure white christening gown in Swiss voile features panels of Swiss lace insertion and delicate lace edging at neckline and sleeves. There is also a lace-trimmed bonnet to match and a petticoat, charmingly embroidered with the name and birth date of each tiny wearer. Although a gown such as this will take a little time, modern sewing machines make the techniques remarkably straightforward.

Petticoat Embroidery Outlines

Christening Gown, Bonnet and Petticoat

Measurements

To fit baby 3 to 6 months old.
Finished length: ***Gown*** *86cm;* ***Petticoat*** *85cm.* ***Bonnet*** *measures approximately 34cm x 17cm when flat.*

Materials

- 1.7m x 115cm white Swiss voile, for Gown and Bonnet
- 1.8m x 115cm white batiste, for Petticoat
- 3.5m x 25mm-wide Swiss lace edging, with entredeux edge
- 2.5m x 20mm-wide Swiss lace insertion
- 2m x 80mm-wide Swiss lace insertion
- 8.7m x 10mm-wide Swiss beading, with entredeux edges
- 4.6m x 3mm-wide entredeux
- 12.3m x 5mm white satin ribbon
- 0.65m x 15mm-wide French lace edging, for Gown
- 1.2m x 10mm-wide French lace edging, for Petticoat
- DMC 50 Broder Machine Thread: white
- Size 60 machine needles
- Shirring elastic
- Four x 8mm-diameter pearl buttons, for Gown
- Two x 12mm-diameter pearl buttons, for Petticoat
- Spray starch
- Size 10 crewel needle
- Stranded Embroidery Cotton: white

Pattern pieces

All pattern pieces, except rectangles and strips, are printed on pattern sheet in pink. Trace Bodice Front 31, Bodice Back 32, Sleeve 33, Armhole Guide 34, Petticoat Front 35, Petticoat Back 36.

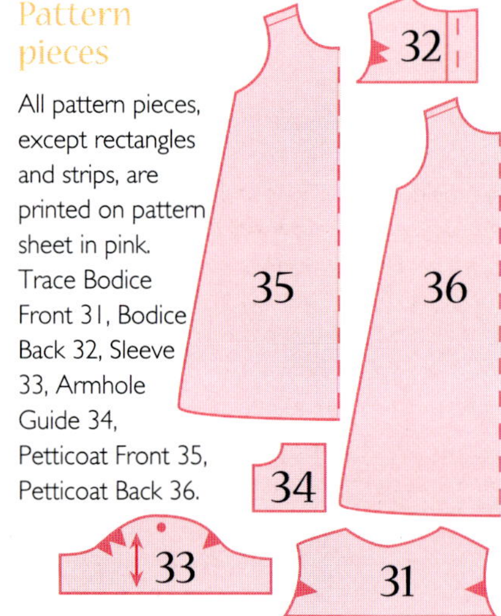

Cutting

NOTE 6mm seam allowance is **included** on all pattern pieces and in all given measurements, unless otherwise specified. It is important that all pieces with a straight edge, such as Skirts, should be cut out on a line marked by pulling a thread in the fabric.

From Swiss voile, cut two Bodice Backs and two Sleeves. Cut also two 15cm squares for Bodice Front Panels, two rectangles, each 52cm long x 95cm wide, for Skirt Back and Front, two strips, each 13.5cm x 95cm, for Lower Skirt Panels, one strip, 2.5cm x 30cm, for Placket, one rectangle, 8.5cm x 35cm, for Bonnet Back, and one strip, 5cm x 70cm, for Bonnet Ruffle.

From batiste, cut one Petticoat Front and one Petticoat Back.

Method

GOWN

1 SKIRT PLACKET (Note that on Skirt rectangles, the long edges are the upper and lower edges; the shorter edges are the sides.) Fold Skirt Back in half along 95cm width, to find centre of upper edge. Very carefully pull a 15cm-long thread from this point to mark Placket slash line. Using a very short stitch length, reinforce area to be slashed by stitching 3mm from either side of pulled thread line, tapering stitching towards lower point, then pivoting on needle and taking one stitch across bottom point. Cut along pulled thread line as far as stitching, taking great care not to cut stitching.

With right sides together and raw edges even, stitch Placket strip to opening with a 5mm seam. Trim seam allowance to 3mm and press towards Placket. Press under 5mm on remaining long raw edge of Placket, then fold pressed edge to inside and slipstitch over seam. Press again, folding righthand edge of Placket to inside along seamline, so that it laps neatly over lefthand edge.

2 SIDE SEAM Join Skirt Front to Skirt Back along *one* side seam only, using one of two methods, as follows: For a French seam, with *wrong* sides together, stitch side seam allowing 3mm seam allowance. Press, pressing both seam allowances in the same direction. Fold fabric, with *right* sides together, along seamline and press again. Stitch to encase raw edges, allowing a 6mm seam. This method will take more than the given 6mm seam

allowance but this will not make any difference to the finished skirt. Alternatively, you can stitch the seam in the usual manner, with right sides together, then trim seam allowance to a scant 3mm and neatly overcast edges together using "roll and whip" (see **Step 3**, below). Press seam towards Back.

Stitch Lower Skirt Panels together at *one* side (13.5cm) seam, using the same method that you used for the Skirt.

3 LACE EDING & INSERTIONS ON SKIRT When joining laces, try to line up the holes on succeeding rows of beading and match patterns on lace edging and insertion. Always start pattern matching at Skirt Front. Press and spray starch all fabrics and laces before stitching.

Measure along lower edge of Skirt. Cut a length of Swiss lace edging to this measurement (A), as well as four lengths of beading (B, C, D, E), one length of 20mm-wide Swiss lace insertion (F), one length of 80mm-wide Swiss lace insertion (G), and four lengths of ribbon (H, I, J, K).

Starting at the lower edge and working upwards, join Swiss laces together in the following manner, pressing well after each addition: With right sides together, entredeux holes aligned, and using a stitch length of 1.5, straight stitch Swiss edging (A) to one length of beading (B), stitching as close to as possible, but not on, the straight woven edge of the entredeux. This is called "stitch-in-the-ditch". Trim the batiste seam allowance back to 3mm, then zigzag the two raw trimmed edges together using a stitch width of 3 and stitch length of 1. The needle should stitch through the seam allowance fabric on the left, and clear the edge of the fabric on the right, forming a small neatly rolled edge. This is called "roll and whip". Press.

Using the same technique, that is, stitch-in-the-ditch, followed by roll and whip, stitch remaining edge of beading (B) to the strip of 20mm-wide insertion (F). Now stitch upper edge of insertion (F) to second strip of beading (C), in the same way, and press.

Next, stitch upper edge of beading (C) to lower edge of Skirt Panel; then upper edge of Skirt Panel to third length of beading (D), then remaining edge of beading (D) to 80mm-wide insertion (G); then upper edge of insertion (G) to fourth length of beading (E). Finally, stitch upper edge of beading (E) to lower edge of Skirt, and press well.

Thread ribbon (H, I, J, K) through beading, from one side to the other.

4 REMAINING SIDE SEAM Join Skirt Front to Skirt Back along remaining side seam, using the method that you used previously, securing ribbon ends at the same time and taking care to match lace seam lines. Press seam towards Back.

5 ARMHOLES Using Gown Armhole Guide, and aligning side seam with edge of Guide, cut armhole curves in Skirt. Stitch two rows of gathering along upper edges of Skirt Front and Skirt Back, 3mm and 6mm from the edge. Set Skirt aside.

6 BODICE FRONT Cut one 10cm length of 20mm-wide insertion (A), two x 10cm lengths of beading (B, C), and two x 10cm lengths of satin ribbon (D, E).

Using the stitch-in-the-ditch method and finishing seams by rolling and whipping, join beading (B, C) to each side of insertion (A), then, matching lower straight edges, join a Bodice Front Panel to each side of beading (B, C) – upper edge of Panels will extend beyond laces. Thread ribbon through beading. Press bodice fabric well.

Place Bodice Front pattern piece over the constructed fabric, matching centre fronts, and cut one Bodice Front.

Cut a length of entredeux to fit along lower edge of Bodice Front. Using stitch-in-the-ditch and roll and whip, attach entredeux to lower edge. Press seam towards Bodice and, to prevent it rolling back, on the outside, topstitch as close as possible to seam, using a short stitch length.

7 BODICE BACK With right sides together, join Bodice Front and Backs at shoulder seams. Roll and whip raw edges of seam and press towards Back.

Fold in raw edges of centre Bodice Backs along fold lines and stitch to form placket.

Cut a length of entredeux to fit along each lower edge of Bodice Back, plus a little extra for turning. Pin entredeux in place, folding in raw ends level with opening edge and aligning holes on inside and outside. Stitch in place and topstitch as for Bodice Front.

8 NECK EDGE Staystitch around neck edge. Cut a length of entredeux to go around neck edge, plus a little extra for turning (approximately 31cm). Cut a piece of 15mm-wide French lace edging 1 1/2 times the length of the entredeux.

To gather edge of lace, either pull up a thread in the heading of the lace or run a gathering thread along the heading and pull up bobbin thread until lace fits entredeux. Trim batiste seam allowance from one side of entredeux. For a really special finish, with right sides together and upper edges even, whipstitch lace to entredeux by hand, stitching through every hole in the entredeux. If you prefer to sew by machine, with right sides both face up, butt the trimmed edge of the entredeux to the gathered edge of the lace and zigzag the edges together, setting the stitch length so that the needle goes into every hole in the entredeux (approximate stitch length 1, width 3).

Clip across batiste seam allowance on remaining side of lace-trimmed entredeux. With right sides together, and allowing a 6mm seam, pin entredeux to neck edge. Fold extending ends level with folded edge, making sure that holes are matching on inside and outside. Join entredeux to neck edge, using stitch-in-the-ditch method. Finish raw edges of seam by rolling and whipping, and press towards Bodice. On right side of Bodice, topstitch close to seam on neck edge, securing seam allowance in stitching. Neatly hand-finish raw ends of lace and entredeux at neck edge.

9 JOINING BODICE TO SKIRT Pull up gathering on upper edges of Skirt Front and Back to fit Bodice Front and Back. With right sides together and entredeux uppermost, baste then stitch Bodice to Skirt, using stitch-in-the-ditch method and checking as you stitch that gathering is even. Make two rows of stitching for reinforcement.

Trim Skirt seam allowance *only* to 3mm. Fold entredeux seam allowance over trimmed Skirt seam allowance, baste and zigzag in place. Slipstitch folded edge of seam allowance to gathers on Skirt, making sure stitching does not show on right side of garment.

10 ARMHOLES Cut two lengths of entredeux to fit armholes (about 32cm each). Using stitch-in-the-ditch method, join a length of entredeux to each armhole, overlapping at underarm. Trim raw edges of seam, then roll and whip, and press towards Bodice. Neatly sew entredeux ends together where they overlap. On right side of Bodice, topstitch close to seam, securing seam allowance in stitching.

11 SLEEVES Cut two x 40cm lengths of Swiss lace edging. Join a length to lower edge of each Sleeve, using stitch-in-the-ditch method and finishing by rolling and whipping. Press seam allowance towards Sleeve and topstitch close to seam, catching seam allowance in stitching.

Stitch two rows of gathering between notches on upper edge of Sleeve.

Cut two lengths of shirring elastic, approximately 40cm each. Beginning at underarm seam edge, zigzag (stitch length 2; width 2) over elastic, positioning it 1.2cm from lower edge of each Sleeve. Pull up ends of shirring elastic to fit baby's arm (not too tight) and tie ends together to secure.

Stitch underarm seams of Sleeves using a French seam (see **Step 2**, on page 30), securing ends of elastic at the same time.

Pull up gathers on Sleeves to fit entredeux in armholes. With right sides together, pin Sleeves to armhole edges, with centre dot at shoulder seam and matching notches and underarm seams. Adjust gathering, concentrating gathers at top of Sleeve. Baste and stitch-in-the-ditch, roll and whip raw edges of seam and press towards Sleeves.

12 FINISHING Make four evenly spaced buttonholes in right side Placket of Bodice Back, by hand or machine. Sew buttons on left side Placket to correspond.

Cut a 1.4m length of satin ribbon, tie into a small bow in the middle and handsew to Skirt Front below centre front Bodice. Cut two more lengths of ribbon, each 30cm, and tie into small bows. Handsew a bow to gathering line on lower edge of each Sleeve.

BONNET

1 BACK Cut two x 35cm lengths of beading (A, B), and one 35cm length of 20mm-wide Swiss lace insertion (C). Using stitch-in-the-ditch method and finishing raw edges by rolling and whipping (as for **Step 3**, of Gown, page 31), join beading (A) to one long raw edge of Bonnet Back; join beading (A) to lace insertion (C); then join insertion (C) to remaining length of beading (B). Cut a 35cm length of 5mm-wide satin ribbon and thread it through the beading attached to Bonnet Back, basting across raw ends to hold in place.

2 RUFFLE Cut a 70cm length of 25mm-wide Swiss lace edging and join to one long raw edge of Ruffle, using stitch-in-the-ditch method. Trim, then roll and whip raw edges of seam, and press towards Ruffle. Run two rows of gathering along remaining long raw edge of Ruffle.

3 JOINING RUFFLE TO BACK Pull up gathering to fit Bonnet Back. With right sides together, and entredeux on beading uppermost, baste then stitch Back to gathered edge of Ruffle, using stitch-in-the-ditch method and checking as you stitch that gathering is evenly distributed. Trim seam allowance, then roll and whip for neat finish.

4 FINISHING Press under and handstitch a narrow hem along the raw edge on each side of Bonnet.

Press under 5mm, then another 1cm, along remaining long raw edge of Bonnet Back, and stitch to form casing. Cut a 130cm length of 5mm ribbon and thread through beading attached to Ruffle, leaving ends extending evenly at each end. Cut an 80cm length of 5mm ribbon, thread through casing on back edge, draw up tightly and tie in a bow.

PETTICOAT

1 EMBROIDERY (Work embroidery on Petticoat before making up.) Embroidery outlines are printed on page 28. Trace onto tracing paper and mark main features *very lightly* on Petticoat Front with a small dot, using a water soluble pen or sharp 2B pencil, positioning the smaller motif just below neckline and the larger motif just above the lower hem.

Referring to the **Embroidery Stitch Guide** on page 112, embroider designs. Using one strand of embroidery cotton, shadow stitch ribbon outlines. Add roses and buds in bullion stitch. A charming touch is to embroider the dressmaker's name as well as the name and date of birth of the baby along the lefthand edge of the hem, leaving space along the hem to embroider the names of the many babies to follow!

2 JOINING FRONT TO BACK Stitch Front to Back at sides, using French seams or a narrow straight seam, finished with roll and whip. Press seam towards Back.

3 LACE TRIMS Beginning at one underarm seam and using stitch-in-the-ditch method, join entredeux to neck and armhole edges, clipping into seam allowance on entredeux to ease it around curves of shoulder straps. Overlap ends at underarm and finish neatly by hand. Trim, then roll and whip raw edges of seam, and press towards garment. On right side of Petticoat, topstitch close to entredeux seam, catching seam allowance in stitching.

Trim batiste seam allowance from remaining edge of entredeux. Beginning at same underarm seam, butt 10mm lace edging up to entredeux and zigzag in place, following method described in **Step 8** of Gown, page 31. Use a pin to pull a thread in the lace heading to gather it slightly around the curves of the shoulder straps. Zigzag over underarm join to neaten.

Finish lower edge with entredeux and 30mm-wide lace edging.

4 FINISHING Work a buttonhole by hand or machine in each Back shoulder strap, then sew buttons on Front shoulder strap to correspond.

sweet DREAMS

Hand-finished with shell stitch edging and bullion stitch roses, this exquisite nightgown is an ideal gift for a new baby girl. Simple to sew, in a classic and much loved style, the complete layette features matching bonnet, matinée jacket and pilchers as well. To complement the garments, we've also added a cuddly crocheted bunny rug and a baby-sized teddy bear that can be knitted in no time. Instructions begin over the page.

Nightgown

Measurements

To fit baby up to 6 months.
Finished length approximately 48cm.

Materials

- 1.1m x 112cm cream fabric, such as Vyella, Clydella or other wool/cotton mix
- DMC Stranded Embroidery Cotton in following colours and amounts: two skeins v. lt shell pink 224, one skein each green-grey 3053, lt blue-violet 341 and pale dusty rose 963
- 0.6m bias binding (purchased or self-made)
- Five 10mm buttons
- 1.5m x 5mm pink satin ribbon

Pattern pieces

Pattern pieces are printed on pattern sheet in pink. Trace Front/Back 37, Sleeve 38 and Neck Binding 39.

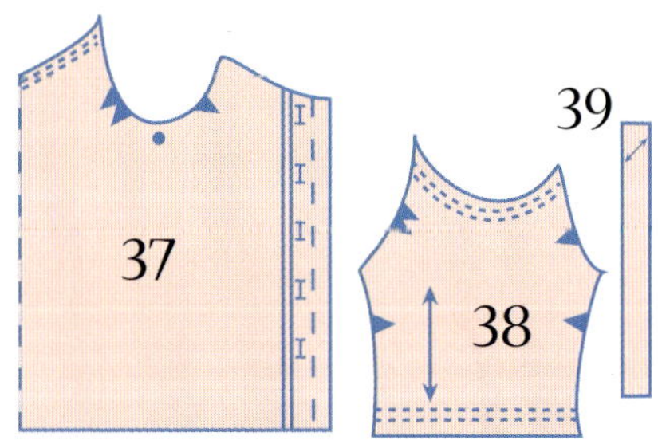

Cutting

NOTE 1cm seam allowance is **included** on all pieces unless otherwise indicated, as well as 3cm hem allowance on lower edge and 5mm on Sleeve.

From fabric, cut one Front/Back, two Sleeves and one Neck Binding (on the bias).

Method

Unless otherwise indicated, all seams are stitched with right sides together.

1 SLEEVES Mark buttonholes onto right side of lower Sleeves, as indicated on pattern, and stitch by hand or machine. Stitch underarm seam of each Sleeve and neaten raw edge. Alternatively, complete this step using a French seam.

2 RAGLAN SEAMS Stitch Sleeves to nightgown, matching symbols. Neaten raw edges. Alternatively, complete this step using a French seam.

3 FRONT PLACKET On right Front of nightgown, bring wrong sides together and stitch on indicated lines to make narrow tuck for placket. Press tuck away from centre front. Press under 5mm allowance on raw edge of right Front and machine-stitch close to folded edge. Fold placket to inside along given fold line and slipstitch hemmed edge invisibly along tuck line. Press. To complete placket, topstitch 4mm from front edge, matching stitching on tuck.

4 FRONT FACING On left Front, press under 5mm allowance on raw edge and machine-stitch close to folded edge. Fold facing to inside along given fold line and press. Slipstitch hemmed edge invisibly to inside front. On the outside, topstitch close to the front edge.

5 NECK BINDING Run gathering threads around neck edge and draw up gathers to fit Neck Binding, allowing Binding to extend 1cm at either end. With raw edges even, baste and stitch Binding to neck edge. Fold Binding around to inside, turn under raw edge (including ends) and handstitch in place over seam with tiny stitches.

6 SLEEVE CASING Press under 5mm and handsew a narrow hem on lower edges of Sleeves. Cut two pieces of bias binding to fit around casing circumference of Sleeve, allowing a small amount extra for turning in raw ends. Stitch bias binding in place on inside of each Sleeve to form casing, following stitching lines given on pattern and making sure that buttonhole is centred in each casing.

7 HEM Press up hem on lower edge of gown, turn in raw edge and slipstitch invisibly in place.

8 BUTTONHOLES Work five evenly-spaced buttonholes in placket, as indicated on pattern, and sew on five buttons to correspond. Press garment before beginning embroidery.

9 EMBROIDERY With three strands of 224 embroidery thread and following **Embroidery Stitch Guide** on page 112, work shell stitch along both edges of placket, around neck edge and along lower edge of Sleeves.

Using photograph, above, as a guide, and **Embroidery Stitch Guide** on page 112, with one strand of cotton, work bullion stitch roses and buds in 224 and 963, satin stitch leaves in 3053 and French knot forget-me-nots in 341 evenly between buttonholes.

10 FINISHING Cut two 50cm lengths of ribbon and thread through casing on Sleeves. Tie remaining 50cm ribbon into a little bow, trim ends (so baby can't get them in her mouth or round her neck) and stitch firmly to neck edge at centre front.

Matinée Jacket

Measurements

To fit baby up to 6 months.

Materials

- 0.6m x 112cm cream fabric, such as Vyella, Clydella or other wool/cotton mix
- 0.6m x 112cm printed fabric for lining (a plain coloured silk is also very pretty)
- DMC Stranded Embroidery Cotton in the following colours and amounts: two skeins v. lt shell pink 224, one skein each green-grey 3053, lt blue-violet 341 and pale dusty rose 963
- One 10mm button
- 1m x 5mm pink satin ribbon

Pattern piece

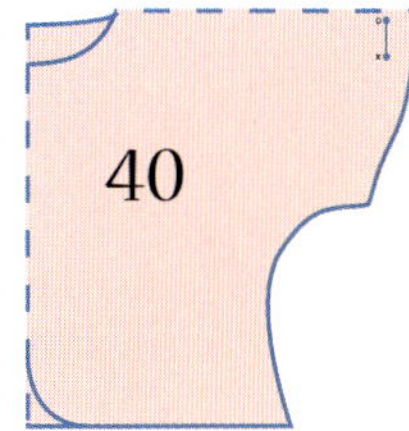

Pattern piece is printed on pattern sheet in pink. Trace Jacket Front/Back 40.

Cutting

NOTE 5mm seam allowance is **included** around all edges. Jacket is cut in one piece. Fold fabric in half, then half again, so that centre front/back and shoulder can be positioned along fold lines. When basic outline has been cut out, unfold jacket and cut centre front opening, as well as neckline and rounded corners.

From cream fabric, cut one Front/Back, as above.

From lining fabric, cut one Front/Back, as above.

Method

Unless otherwise indicated, all seams are stitched with right sides together.

1 UNDERARM/SIDE SEAM Stitch underarm/side seam on both jacket and lining. Clip curves, turn right side out and press.

2 EMBROIDERY Following **Embroidery Stitch Guide** on page 112, using photograph as a guide to placement, and using one strand of embroidery thread, work bullion stitch roses and buds, satin stitch leaves and French knot forget-me-nots, as for nightgown, around the curved lower front edges.

3 JOINING JACKET TO LINING Stitch jacket and lining together around all edges except Sleeves. Clip curves and turn right side out. Tack along edges to hold shape and press.

4 SLEEVE PLEATS Press under seam allowance on Sleeve and lining edges, then form a small inverted pleat, as indicated on pattern, on both Sleeve and lining, and baste to hold. Handsew edges together with tiny stitches, securing pleat at same time. Press. Trim pleats on Sleeves with small bows.

5 EDGING With three strands of 224 embroidery cotton, work shell stitch around all edges (see **Embroidery Stitch Guide** on page 112).

6 FINISHING Sew loop and button at neck edge, and trim with ribbon.

Pilchers

Measurements

To fit baby up to 6 months.

Materials

- 0.4m x 112cm cream fabric, such as Vyella, Clydella or other wool/cotton mix
- 0.4m x 112cm printed fabric for lining
- One skein DMC Stranded Embroidery Cotton in each of the following colours: v. lt shell pink 224, green-grey 3053, lt blue-violet 341 and pale dusty rose 963
- Eight metal stud poppers
- 0.5m x 5mm pink satin ribbon

Pattern piece

Pattern piece is printed on pattern sheet in pink. Trace Pilchers Front/Back 41.

Cutting

NOTE 5mm seam allowance is **included** around all edges.

From cream fabric, cut one Front/Back.

From lining fabric, cut one Front/Back.

Method

Unless otherwise indicated, all seams are stitched with right sides together.

1 EMBROIDERY Using the photograph as a guide to placement, and using one strand of embroidery thread, work bullion stitch roses and buds, satin stitch leaves and French knot forget-me-nots, as for nightgown, around the curved front edges of pilchers.

2 DARTS Stitch darts in front and back of both pilchers and lining.

3 JOINING PILCHERS & LINING Stitch Pilchers and lining together around all edges, leaving open for turning between notches, as indicated. Clip curves, turn right side out, close opening and press.

4 POPPERS Insert four metal stud poppers into each side of pilchers, as indicated.

5 EDGING With three strands of 224 embroidery cotton, work shell stitch around all edges (see **Embroidery Stitch Guide** on page 112).

6 FINISHING Trim centre front with a small pink bow.

Bonnet

Measurements

To fit baby up to 6 months.

Materials

- 0.2m x 112cm cream fabric, such as Vyella, Clydella or other wool/cotton mix
- 0.2m x 112cm printed fabric for lining
- One skein DMC Stranded Embroidery Cotton in each of the following colours: v. lt shell pink 224, green-grey 3053, lt blue-violet 341 and pale dusty rose 963
- 1m x 10mm satin ribbon

Pattern pieces

Pattern pieces are printed on pattern sheet in pink. Trace Bonnet 42, Crown 43 and Brim 44.

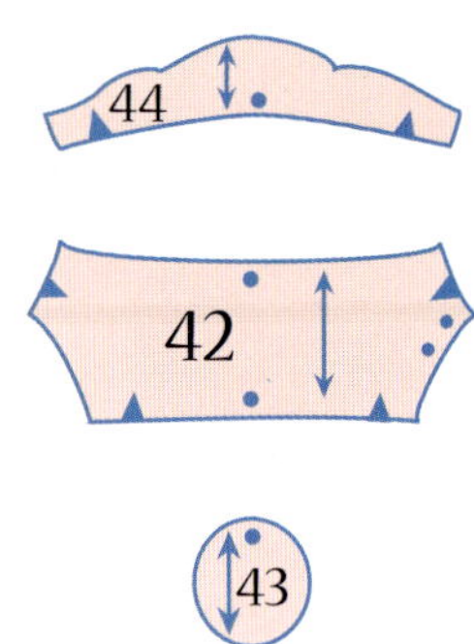

Cutting

NOTE 5mm seam allowance is **included** around all edges.

From cream fabric cut one Bonnet, one Crown and two Brims.

From lining, cut one Bonnet and one Crown.

Method

Unless otherwise indicated, all seams are stitched with right sides together.

1 EMBROIDERY Using the photograph as a guide to placement, **Embroidery Stitch Guide** on page 112, and using one strand of embroidery thread, work bullion stitch roses and buds, satin stitch leaves and French knot forget-me-nots, as for nightgown, along the centre of one Brim (Brim lining).

2 JOINING BRIM TO BONNET Run a line of ease stitching along brim (front) edge of Bonnet. Pin non-embroidered Brim to Bonnet and adjust ease stitching if necessary. Stitch as pinned.

3 CENTRE BACK SEAM Stitch centre back seam of Bonnet.

4 CROWN Run a line of gathering thread around back edge of Bonnet and draw up gathers to fit Crown. Pin Crown to Bonnet, adjusting gathers evenly around Crown, and stitch as pinned.

5 BONNET LINING Stitch Bonnet lining as for Bonnet, **Steps 2 to 4**, above.

6 JOINING BONNET TO LINING With right sides together pin Bonnet to lining around raw edges and stitch, leaving a small opening in neck edge, as indicated. Clip curves and turn right side out through opening. Slipstitch opening closed and press, pushing lining into bonnet. Align Brim seams and take a couple of tiny invisible stitches through both layers to secure.

7 EDGING With three strands of 224 embroidery cotton, work shell stitch around all edges (see **Embroidery Stitch Guide** on page 112).

8 FINISHING Fold Brim back over bonnet so that embroidery is on the outside. Sew a ribbon tie to each side of bonnet, as indicated. Decorate sides of bonnet with small bows or multiple ribbon loops and bullion stitch roses.

Crocheted Baby Rug

Measurements

Finished rug measures 102cm square.

Materials

Patons 3-ply Fairytale (25g):

- **Main Colour** (MC, white): 7 balls
- **1st Contrast** (C1, pale blue): 5 balls
- **2nd Contrast** (C2, pale pink): 3 balls
- One 5.00mm (Size 6) crochet hook

Tension

See **Knitting and Crochet Notes** on page 120. Square should measure 12cm x 12cm, using 5.00mm hook. To achieve desired effect, rug has been designed to be worked on a bigger hook and at a looser tension than is usually recommended.

SQUARE (make 64)

Using MC and 5.00mm hook, make 6ch.
1st row. Miss 3ch, 1tr in each of next 3ch, *turn.*
2nd row. 6ch, miss 3 of these ch, 1tr in each of next 3ch, (sl st, 3ch, 3tr) in 3ch loop at end of previous row, *turn.*
3rd row. 6ch, miss 3 of these ch, 1tr in each of next 3ch, (sl st, 3ch, 3tr) in each 3ch loop to end (3 patts). *Turn.*
Rep 3rd row 4 times…(7 patts).
Fasten off.
Join in C1 and rep 3rd row once…(8 patts).
9th row. Using C1, sl st across first 3tr, (sl st, 3ch, 3tr) in each 3ch loop to last loop, sl st in last loop. Fasten off (7 patts).
10th row. Join C2 with a sl st in first 3ch loop, 3ch, 3tr in same loop, (sl st, 3ch, 3tr) in each 3ch loop to last loop, sl st in last loop (6 patts).
11th row. Using C2, as 9th row (5 patts).
Working in stripes of 1 row each C1 and C2, then 2 rows C1, cont dec in this manner, in each row until 1 patt rem. Fasten off.

To make up

Do not press. With MC half of each square in the upper left corner, arrange pieces into 8 rows of 8 squares each. Holding 2 squares with right sides facing and working through both thicknesses, join MC with a sl st in corner, 1ch, 1dc in same place as sl st, *2ch, 1dc between patts, rep from * to end, working last dc in corner. Fasten off.

Cont joining squares tog until you have 8 strips of 8 squares, then join strips together in the same manner.

BORDER

With right side facing, join MC with a sl st in corner, 1ch, *3dc in corner, (2ch, 1dc between patts) along edge to next corner, rep from * 3 times, sl st in first dc.
2nd rnd. Using MC, 3ch, *3tr in centre st of corner, 1tr in next dc, 3tr in each 2ch sp to next corner, 1tr in next dc, rep from * 3 times (omitting 1dc at end of last rep), sl st in top of 3ch. Fasten off.
3rd rnd. Join C1 in any corner st, 1ch, *(1dc, 2ch, 1dc) in corner st, (1ch, miss 1tr, 1dc in next tr) to next corner st, rep from * 3 times, sl st in first dc. Fasten off.
4th rnd. Join C2 in any corner sp, 1ch, *(1dc, 2ch, 1dc) in corner sp, (1ch, 1dc in next sp) to next corner, 1ch, rep from * 3 times, sl st in first dc. Fasten off.
Working in stripes of 1 rnd each C1, C2, C1 and MC, rep 4th round 4 times. Do not fasten off at end of last rnd.
9th rnd. Using MC, 3ch, *5tr in corner sp, (1tr in next dc, 1tr in next sp) to next corner, 1tr in next dc, rep from * 3 times, (omitting 1tr at end of last rep), sl st in top of 3ch. Fasten off.

Knitted Teddy

Measurements

Finished teddy is approximately 12cm tall.

Materials

Patons 4-ply Feathersoft (25g):

- One ball (makes two Teddies)
- One pair 3.00mm (No 11) knitting needles
- Washable filling
- Stranded cotton for embroidered features
- Tapestry needle for embroidery and sewing seams
- Length of narrow ribbon

Tension

See **Knitting and Crochet Notes** on page 120.
31 sts and 41 rows to 10cm over st st, using 3.00mm needles.

TEDDY (make 2)

First Leg. Cast on 7 sts.
Work in st st, inc one st at each end of 3rd row, then at beg of alt rows 3 times…12 sts.
Work one row.
Break off yarn.
Second Leg. On the end of the needle holding the First Leg sts, cast on 7 sts.
Work to correspond with First Leg (reversing shaping), but do not break off yarn.
11th row (joining Legs). K2tog, knit across Second Leg to last st, inc one st in last st, knit across First Leg to last 2 sts, K2tog…23 sts.
Work 9 rows st st, dec one st at each end of 6th row…21 sts.
Shape for Arms. Cont in st st, inc one st at each end of next 4 rows, then cast on 3 sts at beg of foll 2 rows…35 sts.
Work 4 rows st st.
Shape top of Arms. Cast off 10 sts at beg of next 2 rows…15 sts.
Shape Head. Inc one st at each end of next and foll alt rows until there are 21 sts.
Work 7 rows st st.
Dec one st at each end of next row.
Work one row.
Dec one st at each end of every row until 11 sts rem.
Cast off.

EAR (make 2)

Cast on 9 sts.
Work in st st, dec one st at each end of 3rd row, then in foll alt rows until 3 sts rem.
Inc one st at each end of alt rows until there are 9 sts.
Work one row.
Cast off.

To make up

Do not press. Place body pieces right sides tog, then using back stitch, join tog, leaving cast-off edge open. Turn right side out and fill lightly; close opening. Fold Ears in half with wrong sides tog, oversew edges, then sew Ears to head. Using stranded cotton, and working in cross stitch and straight stitch (see **Embroidery Stitch Guide** on page 112), embroider Teddy's facial features, as photographed. Tie ribbon around neck and stitch in position.

babes in the WOOL

These beautiful handknits are designed to fit babies aged up to 6 months old. But because some little cherubs just can't wait to get here, we've also included three tiny sizes for premature babies. The set on this page features a delicate picot edge and bullion stitch roses – perfect for a little girl. The garments opposite are knitted in easy garter stitch, with instructions for both 4-ply and 8-ply wool. *Knitting instructions begin on page107.*

colour by NUMBERS

Here's a delightful first book that can't be torn, as a younger baby explores the soft felt pages and an older tot learns to count the colourful images. Made entirely from felt – which comes in a wonderful array of hand-washable colours – the outlines are stitched in place with simple running stitch, then highlighted with extra hand-embroidery. Of course, if you prefer, the sewing machine can be used to speed things up.

One tree with one red apple ...

Two flowers, each with two leaves ...

Three fat hens, with three tiny speckles ...

Four slippery snakes with four spots …

Five branches with five green leaves …

Six fluffy clouds …

Seven pretty butterflies …

Eight fat coloured pencils …

Nine hearts (can you find the red one?) …

And ten stars twinkling in the night sky.

Felt Counting Book

Measurements

Finished book is 17.5cm square.

Materials

- Felt in the following colours and amounts: bright yellow, orange, sky blue and medium blue (each 20cm square), light brown, turquoise, bright blue and jacaranda blue (each 25cm x 20cm), pale yellow, mauve and grass green (each 25cm x 35cm), red and dark blue (each 10cm square), flesh colour, purple and lime green (each 10cm x 30cm), rust brown and white (each 15cm square)
- 30cm narrow strip dark blue felt, for Bookmark (this could also be several strands of thick wool or 30cm blue cord, if preferred)
- Transfer paper
- Temporary fabric glue, such as No More Pins
- Machine thread to match felt colours
- Fabric paint: white, blue and brown

Appliqué outlines

All outlines, including numbers, are printed on pages 42 to 45. Trace each outline onto tracing paper, including any separate sections for composite images, such as the Centre of the Flower, the Apple on the Tree, the Snake's Tongue, the Hen's Beak and Comb.

Method

1 BACKGROUND PAGES & SPINE From pale yellow felt, cut two 17.5cm squares; from each of the following colours, cut one 17.5cm square: light brown, grass green, turquoise, bright blue, medium blue, sky blue, jacaranda blue and mauve (10 squares in all, which will form the "pages" of the book).

From each of the following colours, cut one 17.5cm x 2.5cm rectangle: bright yellow, turquoise, bright blue, jacaranda blue and purple (five rectangles in all, which will form the "spine" of the book).

2 GENERAL APPLIQUÉ INSTRUCTIONS Following the specific instructions in **Step 3**, below, transfer the appliqué outlines to the appropriately coloured felt using transfer paper and cut out carefully. Generally, the pieces are cut without any seam allowance, but where one piece is overlapped by another, such as the Snake's Tongue or the Hen's Beak, you should add 5mm allowance to the edge that is overlapped, so that it can be tucked beneath the top piece. Where the pieces would be really tiny if you cut them separately, you can sometimes cut them in one piece to make things easier. For example, it would be simpler to cut the Butterfly Wings as a single piece and appliqué the body over the top; similarly, the Pencil can be cut in one piece from bottom to point, and the flesh-coloured Sharpened Section can be appliquéd on top.

Using the photograph as a guide to placement, fix the pieces in position with a sparing dab of glue, remembering to allow for overlapping where appropriate. Then stitch each piece in place using a small running stitch about 2mm from the edge. This can be done on the sewing machine if you prefer, although you might find some of the small pieces too fiddly.

Details can be traced into place with transfer paper, if necessary, then filled in with fabric paint in the appropriate colour.

3 APPLIQUÉ SHAPES Cut each shape as follows: PAGE 1 TREE: Background page is pale yellow, cut Number One from jacaranda blue, Apple from red, Tree Canopy from grass green, Trunk from rust brown, Hollow from light brown, paint apple stalk in brown; PAGE 2 FLOWERS: Background page is bright blue, cut Number Two from dark blue, Flower Petals from orange, Flower Centres from bright yellow, Stalks from grass green, Leaves from lime green, paint dots around flower centres in blue; PAGE 3 HENS: Background page is light brown, cut Number Three from jacaranda blue, Hens from flesh colour, Combs and Wattles from red, Beaks from rust brown, paint eyes in white, pupils and line on Beak in blue, and speckles in brown; PAGE 4 SNAKES: Background page is turquoise, cut Number Four from lime green, Snakes from mauve, Snake Tongues from orange, paint eyes in white, pupils in blue and dots in brown; PAGE 5 BRANCHES: Background page is grass green, cut Number Five from dark blue, Branches from rust brown (because they are very thin, use diagonal overcasting to stitch them to the background), Leaves from lime green; PAGE 6 CLOUDS: Background page is jacaranda blue, cut Number Six from pale yellow, Clouds from white; PAGE 7 BUTTERFLIES: Background page is medium blue, cut Number Seven from rust brown, Butterfly Bodies from lime green, Wings from each of bright yellow, orange, light brown, jacaranda blue, dark blue, purple and mauve, paint eyes in white, pupils in blue and antennae in brown; PAGE 8 PENCILS: Background page is mauve, cut Number Eight in light brown, two Pencils (including Points) from each of grass green, turquoise, jacaranda blue and dark blue, Sharpened Sections from flesh colour, paint stripes in brown; PAGE 9 HEARTS: Background page is pale yellow, cut Number Nine from bright blue, one Heart from red, eight Hearts from orange; PAGE 10 STARS: Background page is sky blue, cut Number Ten from mauve, five Stars from bright yellow, five Stars from pale yellow.

4 ATTACHING SPINE With wrong sides together and using running stitch around all edges, sew the pages to each other in pairs (in numerical order), catching a "spine" rectangle between the lefthand edges, allowing 1.5cm of spine to protrude from finished page. Sew Pages 1 and 2 with a turquoise spine, Pages 3 and 4 with a bright yellow spine, Pages 5 and 6 with a bright blue spine, Pages 7 and 8 with a purple spine and Pages 9 and 10 with a jacaranda blue spine.

5 ASSEMBLING BOOK Lay the completed pages on top of one another in order, with edges and spines even. Stitch the spines together through all layers, stitching about 1cm from the lefthand edge.

6 BOOKMARK If using felt, roll the strip into a tight cord and catch the edge in place along the cord. Tie a knot in each end. If using wool, plait several strands together for extra thickness, and tie a knot in each end. Stitch one end of cord firmly to top of spine.

Tongue
Stalk
Leaf
Flower Petals
Centre
Snake
Tree Canopy
Cloud
Apple
Heart
Point
Sharpened
Section
Butterfly
Body
Wing
Trunk
Pencil
Hollow

hello DOLLIES

Destined to become the darlings of some small person's heart, these lovable little rag dolls are gifts to cherish. The soft towelling dolls on this page are a perfect first toy for a baby – cuddly and washable, they can be sucked and chewed with impunity.

The little rag doll, opposite, would be ideal for a slightly older child. Made from soft rib knit, with knitting wool hair and simple fleecy knit clothes, she'd make a perfect bedtime companion. *Sewing instructions begin on page 95.*

THE TALE OF PETER RABBIT
Hawcock
Plesiosaur
Henry Holt
JANE HISSEY
Old Bear
JANE HISSEY
JANE HISSEY

nursery TALES

Soft, washable, safe and virtually unbreakable, knitted toys make perfect gifts for babies. Any or all of this adorable group would make a very special present indeed, be it the winsome rabbit in overalls or that famous trio, the Three Little Pigs – you surely wouldn't think of knitting just one? *Knitting instructions begin over the page.*

Three Little Pigs

Measurements

Finished height is approximately 28cm.

Materials

Patons Courtelle 8-ply (100g):

- **Main Colour** (M, palest pink): 2 balls

Patons Tasman or Courtelle 8-ply (100g):

- **1st Contrast** (C1, mid blue): small amount
- **2nd Contrast** (C2, crimson): small amount
- **3rd Contrast** (C3, deep yellow): small amount
- **4th Contrast** (C4, cream): small amount
- **5th Contrast** (C5, dark blue): small amount
- **6th Contrast** (C6, pale yellow): small amount
- **7th Contrast** (C7, bright orange-red): small amount
- One pair each 4.00mm (No 8) and 3.00mm (No 11) knitting needles
- Two stitch-holders
- Tapestry needle
- Strong thread, for sewing
- Washable polyester filling
- Five 3cm-diameter plastic joints (per pig)
- Red pencil (optional)
- One skein each brown, rust and white stranded cotton, for embroidery

Tension

See **Knitting and Crochet Notes** on page 120.
26 sts and 34 rows to 10cm over stocking st, using 3.00mm needles *AND* 22 sts and 30 rows to 10cm over stocking st, using 4.00mm needles.

To achieve the desired effect, the pigs have been designed to be worked on smaller needles and at a tighter tension than usually recommended.

PIG (make 3)

BODY (make 2 per pig)

Using 3.00mm needles and M, cast on 12 sts.
1st row (wrong side). Knit.
2nd row. Inc in first st, purl to end.
3rd row. Inc in first st, knit to end.
Rep 2nd and 3rd rows 3 times, then 2nd row once...21 sts.
11th row. Knit, inc 2 sts in centre.
12th row. Purl.
Rep 11th and 12th rows 4 times...31 sts.
Work 10 rows stocking st.
Dec one st at beg of every row until 11 sts rem.
Cast off loosely.

LEGS (make 2 per pig)

Using 3.00mm needles and M, cast on 18 sts.
Work 2 rows stocking st.
3rd row. (Inc once in each of next 2 sts, K5, inc once in each of next 2 sts) twice...26 sts.
4th row. Purl.
5th row. (Inc once in each of next 2 sts, K9, inc once in each of next 2 sts) twice...34 sts.
Work 7 rows stocking st, beg with a purl row.
13th row. K12, (K2tog) 5 times, K12...29 sts.
14th row. Purl.
15th row. K7, (K3tog) 5 times, K7...19 sts.
Work 3 rows stocking st, beg with a purl row.
19th row. Knit, inc one st in centre...20 sts.
Work 13 rows stocking st, beg with a purl row, AT SAME TIME, inc at each end of 2nd and foll 4th rows 3 times in all, then in foll alt row once...28 sts.
33rd row. (K2, sl 1, K1, psso, K1, K2tog) 4 times...20 sts.
34th row. Purl.
35th row. (Sl 1, K1, psso, K1, K2tog) 4 times...12 sts.
36th row. (P2tog) 6 times...6 sts.
Break off yarn, run end through rem sts, draw up tightly and fasten off securely.

ARMS (make 2 per pig)

Using 3.00mm needles and M, cast on 8 sts.
Work 2 rows stocking st (1st row is wrong side).
3rd row. Inc once in each of next 8 sts...16 sts.
4th row. Purl.
5th row. K2, (inc in next st, K1, inc in next st) 4 times, K2...24 sts.
Work 7 rows stocking st, beg with a purl row.
13th row. K2tog, knit to last 2 sts, K2tog.
Work 5 rows stocking st, beg with a purl row.
Rep last 6 rows twice...18 sts.
Shape thumb. 1st row. K8, (inc 2 sts in next st) twice, K8...22 sts.
Work 3 rows stocking st, beg with a purl row.
5th row. K8, (K3tog) twice, K8...18 sts.
Work 5 rows stocking st, beg with a purl row.
11th row. (K2tog) 9 times...9 sts.
Break off yarn, run end through rem sts, draw up tightly and fasten off securely.

HEAD

Using 3.00mm needles and M, cast on 11 sts.
Work 2 rows stocking st (1st row is wrong side).
3rd row. Inc once in each of next 11 sts...22 sts.
Work 3 rows stocking st, beg with a purl row.
7th row. (K1, inc in next st) 11 times...33 sts.
Work 3 rows stocking st, beg with a purl row.
11th row. (K2, inc in next st) 11 times...44 sts.
Work 3 rows stocking st, beg with a purl row.
15th row. (K3, inc in next st) 11 times...55 sts.
Work 11 rows stocking st, beg with a purl row.
27th row. (K3, K2tog) 11 times...44 sts.
28th row. Purl.
Divide for right side of head. 1st row. K18, *turn*.
Cont on these 18 sts.
2nd row. P2tog, purl to end...17 sts.
3rd row. Knit to last 2 sts, K2tog...16 sts.
4th row. P2tog, purl to end...15 sts.
5th row. (K3, K2tog) 3 times...12 sts.
Break off yarn, leave these 12 sts on a stitch-holder.
Join M to rem sts.
Shape gusset. 1st row. K8, *turn*.
Cont on these 8 sts and work 3 rows stocking st, beg with a purl row.
5th row. K2tog, knit to last 2 sts, K2tog...6 sts.
Break off yarn, leave these 6 sts on a stitch-holder.
Left side of head. Join M to rem 18 sts and knit to end.
2nd row. Purl to last 2 sts, P2tog...17 sts.
3rd row. K2tog, knit to end...16 sts.
4th row. Purl to last 2 sts, P2tog...15 sts.

5th row. (K3, K2tog) 3 times…12 sts.
Place all sts from stitch-holders on needle and work 3 rows stocking st, beg with a purl row…30 sts.
Next row. (K3, K2tog) 6 times…24 sts.
Work 3 rows stocking st, beg with a purl row.
Next row. (K2, K2tog) 6 times…18 sts.
Work 3 rows stocking st, beg with a purl row.
Cast off loosely.

NOSE

Using 3.00mm needles and M, cast on 4 sts.
Work 2 rows stocking st (1st row is wrong side).
3rd row. Inc in first st, knit to last st, inc in last st…6 sts.
Work 3 rows stocking st, beg with a purl row.
7th row. K2tog, knit to last 2 sts, K2tog…4 sts.
Work 2 rows stocking st, beg with a purl row.
Cast off.

EARS (make 4 per pig)

Using 3.00mm needles and M, cast on 6 sts.
Work 2 rows stocking st (1st row is wrong side).
3rd row. Inc once in each of next 6 sts…12 sts.
Work 5 rows stocking st, beg with a purl row.
Dec one st at beg of every row until 2 sts rem.
Cast off.

TAIL

Using 3.00mm needles and M, cast on 8 sts.
Work 28 rows stocking st (1st row is wrong side).
29th row. (K2, K2tog) twice…6 sts.
30th row. Purl.
31st row. (K1, K2tog) twice…4 sts.
32nd row. Purl.
Break off yarn, run end through rem sts, draw up tightly and fasten off securely.

To make up

With right sides tog, using a flat seam, and noting that purl side is right side of fabric, join Body pieces tog, leaving an opening at back. Stitch Head and snout gusset tog, join the seam under the Head, leaving a 3cm opening at the back. Join Nose to end of snout. Turn Head right side out and stuff with filling. Join Head and Body using plastic joint pieces as follows: insert one half of joint into both Head and Body, pull up gathers around the joints and fasten off, then snap the joints tog, thus connecting the Head and Body. With right sides tog, join Ear pieces tog in pairs. Fold a pleat in the front of each Ear and stitch Ears in place. With right sides tog, fold Legs and stitch seams, leaving an opening. With right sides tog, fold Arms and stitch seams, leaving an opening. Attach Arms and Legs to Body, using plastic joints, then stuff the limbs and Body with filling and stitch all openings. With right sides tog, fold Tail in half lengthwise and join seam. Using strong thread, run a line of small gathering stitches along the Tail within the seam allowance, next to stitched seamline. Turn Tail right side out. To make Tail curl, pull up gathering thread and fasten off securely. Attach Tail to Body. **Face:** Mark position of eyes. With a strong thread take a stitch through the pig's nose from the eye, straight down to the chin, then back up to the second eye and down to the chin again, pulling the thread slightly to create an eye socket. Using brown stranded embroidery thread and satin stitch (see **Embroidery Stitch Guide** on page 112), work eyes. Add eyelashes in brown straight stitch. Add a tiny white stitch to the centre of each eye, for highlights. Using rust cotton, work two small single straight stitches on Nose for each nostril. Using rust cotton and stem stitch, work mouth. Blush cheeks lightly with red pencil. Using M, work a single vertical stitch down centre of each hand and foot, pulling slightly, to create cloven hoofs.

BLUE SWEATER WITH SAILOR COLLAR

BACK

Using 4.00mm needles and C1, cast on 35 sts.
1st row. K2, *P1, K1, rep from * to last st, K1.
2nd row. K1, *P1, K1, rep from * to end.
3rd row. As 1st row.
Work 5 rows stocking st, beg with a purl row.
Dec one st at beg of next 4 rows…31 sts.
Shape armholes. Cast off 2 sts at beg of next 2 rows…27 sts.**
Work 9 rows stocking st.
Shape shoulders. Next row. P7, K1, (P1, K1) 6 times, P7.
Next row. K7, cast off next 13 sts loosely, K7.
Cont on last 7 sts for left shoulder.
Work 2 rows stocking st.
Cast off.
Join C1 to rem 7 sts for right shoulder.
Work 2 rows stocking st.
Cast off.

FRONT

Work as for Back to **.
Beg stripes. 1st row. K13C1, K1C4, K13C1.
2nd row. P12C1, P3C4, P12C1.
3rd row. Using C1, knit.
4th row. P10C1, P7C4, P10C1.
5th row. K9C1, K9C4, K9C1.
6th row. Using C1, purl.
7th row. K7C1, K13C4, K7C1.
8th row. P6C1, P15C4, P6C1.
9th row. Using C1, K7, P1, (K1, P1) 6 times, K7.
Shape shoulders. Using C1 for rem, complete as for Back.

SLEEVES

Using 4.00mm needles and C1, cast on 23 sts.
Work 3 rows rib as for Back.
4th row. Purl.
Using C5, work 2 rows stocking st.
Using C1 for rem, work 12 rows stocking st.
Cast off loosely.

COLLAR

Using 4.00mm needles and C4, cast on 27 sts.
Knit 14 rows garter st.
15th row. K7, cast off 13 sts loosely, K7.
Cont on last 7 sts and knit 8 rows garter st.
Dec one st at beg of next and alt rows until 2 sts rem.
Cast off.
Join C4 to rem 7 sts and knit 9 rows garter st.
Dec one st at beg of next and alt rows until 2 sts rem.
Cast off.

BOW

Using 4.00mm needles and C5, cast on 5 sts.
Knit 10 rows garter st.
Cast off.

To make up

Using backstitch, join shoulder, side and Sleeve seams. Sew in Sleeves. Stitch Collar to Front, following line of stripes. Stitch Bow in place just below stripes, as pictured.

YELLOW SWEATER WITH SAIL BOAT MOTIF

BACK AND FRONT (alike)

Work as for Back and Front of **Blue Sweater**, using C6 in place of C1, and omitting stripe pattern on Front.

SLEEVES

Using 4.00mm needles and C6, cast on 23 sts.
Work 3 rows rib as for Back.
4th row. Purl.
Change to C4.
5th row. Knit.
Change to C5.
6th row. Purl.
Change to C4.
7th row. Knit.
Using C6 for rem, work 11 rows stocking st, beg with a purl row.
Cast off loosely.

To make up

Using knitting stitch (see **Embroidery Stitch Guide** on page 112), embroider boat from Graph, below, to Front of Sweater as pictured. Using backstitch, join shoulder, side and Sleeve seams. Sew in Sleeves.

Graph for Sail Boat Motif

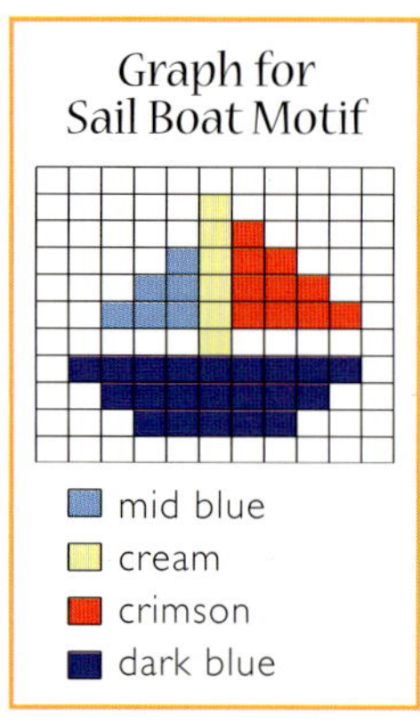

RED SWEATER WITH SAILOR COLLAR

BACK

Work as for Back of **Blue Sweater**, using C7 in place of C1.

FRONT

Work as for Back of **Blue Sweater** to **, using C7 in place of C1.
Divide for vee neck. Next row. K13, *turn*.
***Cont on these 13 sts.
Dec at neck edge in every row until 7 sts rem.
Work 4 rows stocking st.
Cast off.***
Join C7 to rem sts, K2tog, knit to end.
Rep from *** to ***.

SLEEVES

Work as for Sleeves of **Blue Sweater**, using C7 in place of C1 and C2 in place of C5.

COLLAR

Work as for Collar of **Blue Sweater**.

BOW

Work as for Bow of **Blue Sweater**, using C2 in place of C5.

PANTS (make 2 pieces)

BACK (beg at first leg)

Using 4.00mm needles and C1 or C7, cast on 16 sts.
Work 4 rows stocking st.**
Using C5 or C2 for rem, work 6 rows stocking st.
Dec at beg of next row and foll alt row...14 sts.
Work 1 row.
Leave rem sts on a stitch-holder.
Second Leg. Work as for First Leg to **.
Dec at end of next row and foll alt row...14 sts.
Work 1 row.
Join Legs. Next row. Knit across 14 sts of second leg, then with right side facing, knit across 14 sts from left leg stitch-holder...28 sts.
Work 7 rows stocking st, beg with a purl row.
Next row. K13, cast off 2 sts (opening for Tail), K13.
Next row. P13, *turn*, cast on 2 sts, *turn*, P13.
Work 8 rows stocking st, dec one st in centre of last row...27 sts.
Waist. Change to 3.00mm needles.
1st row. K2, *P1, K1, rep from * to last st, K1.
2nd row. K1, *P1, K1, rep from * to end.
3rd row. As 1st row.
Cast off in rib.

FRONT

Work as for Back, noting to omit cast off for the Tail.

To make up

Using backstitch, join side and inside leg seams, reversing seam for the 4 rows of contrast colour.

SKIRT

BACK

Using 4.00mm needles and C3, cast on 39 sts.
1st row. K2, *P1, K1, rep from * to last st, K1.
2nd row. K1, *P1, K1, rep from * to end.
3rd row. As 1st row, inc one st in centre...40 sts.
Work 9 rows stocking st, beg with a purl row.
13th row. K19, cast off 2 sts (opening for Tail), K19.
14th row. P19, *turn*, cast on 2 sts, *turn*, P19.
Work 9 rows stocking st.
Next row. (P1, P2tog) 13 times, P1...27 sts.
Waist. Change to 3.00mm needles.
1st row. K2, *P1, K1, rep from * to last st, K1.
2nd row. K1, *P1, K1, rep from * to end.
3rd row. As 1st row.
Cast off in rib.

FRONT

Work as for Back, noting to omit cast off for Tail.

To make up

Using backstitch, join side seams.

Bunny

Measurements

Finished height approximately 28cm.

Materials

Patons Tasman or Courtelle 8-ply (100g):

- **Main Colour** (M, cream): 1 ball
- **1st Contrast Colour** (C1, pink): small amount
- **2nd Contrast Colour** (C2, dark blue): small amount
- One pair each 4.00mm (No 8) and 3.00mm (No 11) knitting needles
- Two stitch-holders
- Tapestry needle
- Strong thread, for sewing
- Washable polyester filling
- Five 3cm-diameter plastic joints
- Red pencil (optional)
- One skein each brown and white stranded embroidery cotton, for embroidery

Tension

See **Knitting and Crochet Notes** on page 120.
26 sts and 34 rows to 10cm over stocking st, using 3.00mm needles *AND* 22 sts and 30 rows to 10cm over stocking st, using 4.00mm needles.
To achieve the desired effect, the Bunny has been designed to be worked on smaller needles and at a tighter tension than usually recommended.

BUNNY

BODY (make 2)

Using 3.00mm needles and M, cast on 12 sts.
1st row (wrong side). Knit.
2nd row. Inc in first st, purl to end.
3rd row. Inc in first st, knit to end.
Rep 2nd and 3rd rows 3 times, then 2nd row once…21 sts.
11th row. Knit, inc 2 sts in centre.
12th row. Purl.
Rep 11th and 12th rows 4 times…31 sts.
Work 10 rows stocking st.
Dec one st at beg of every row until 11 sts rem.
Cast off loosely.

LEGS (make 2)

Using 3.00mm needles and M, cast on 18 sts.
Work 2 rows stocking st.
3rd row. (Inc once in each of next 2 sts, K5, inc once in each of next 2 sts) twice…26 sts.
4th row. Purl.
5th row. (Inc once in each of next 2 sts, K9, inc once in each of next 2 sts) twice…34 sts.
6th row. Purl.
7th row. K12, (K2tog) 5 times, K12…29 sts.
8th row. Purl.
9th row. K7, (K3tog) 5 times, K7…19 sts.
10th row. Purl.
11th row. K5, (K3tog) 3 times, K5…13 sts.
Work 11 rows stocking st, beg with a purl row.
23rd row. Inc once in each of next 13 sts…26 sts.
Work 5 rows stocking st, beg with a purl row.
29th row. Inc in first st, knit to last st, inc in last st…28 sts.
30th row. Purl.
31st row. (K2, sl 1, K1, psso, K1, K2tog) 4 times…20 sts.
32nd row. Purl.
33rd row. (Sl 1, K1, psso, K1, K2tog) 4 times…12 sts.
34th row. (P2tog) 6 times…6 sts.
Break off yarn, run end through rem sts, draw up tightly and fasten off securely.

ARMS (make 2)

Using 3.00mm needles and M, cast on 6 sts.
Work 2 rows stocking st (1st row is wrong side).
3rd row. (Inc in next st, K1) 3 times…9 sts.
4th row. Purl.
5th row. (Inc in next st, K1, inc in next st) 3 times…15 sts.
6th row. Purl.
7th row. Inc in first st, knit to last st, inc in last st…17 sts.
Work 5 rows stocking st, beg with a purl row.
13th row. K2tog, knit to last 2 sts, K2tog.
Work 7 rows stocking st, beg with a purl row.
Rep last 8 rows once…13 sts.
Next row. K5, inc in next st, K1, inc in next st, K5…15 sts.
Work 5 rows stocking st, beg with a purl row.
Next row. K1, (K2tog) 7 times…8 sts.
Break off yarn, run end through rem sts, draw up tightly and fasten off securely.

HEAD

Using 3.00mm needles and M, cast on 11 sts.
Work 2 rows stocking st (1st row is wrong side).
3rd row. Inc once in each of next 11 sts…22 sts.
Work 3 rows stocking st, beg with a purl row.
7th row. (K1, inc in next st) 11 times…33 sts.
Work 3 rows stocking st, beg with a purl row.
11th row. (K2, inc in next st) 11 times…44 sts.
Work 3 rows stocking st, beg with a purl row.
15th row. (K3, inc in next st) 11 times…55 sts.
Work 11 rows stocking st, beg with a purl row.
27th row. (K3, K2tog) 11 times…44 sts.
28th row. Purl.
Divide for right side of head. 1st row. K18, *turn*.
Cont on these 18 sts.
2nd row. P2tog, purl to end…17 sts.
3rd row. Knit to last 2 sts, K2tog…16 sts.
4th row. P2tog, purl to end…15 sts.
5th row. (K3, K2tog) 3 times…12 sts.
Break off yarn, leave these 12 sts on a stitch-holder.
Join M to rem sts.
Shape gusset. 1st row. K8, *turn*.
Cont on these 8 sts and work 3 rows stocking st, beg with a purl row.
5th row. K2tog, knit to last 2 sts, K2tog…6 sts.
Break off yarn, leave these 6 sts on a stitch-holder.
Left side of head. Join M to rem 18 sts and knit to end.
2nd row. Purl to last 2 sts, P2tog…17 sts.
3rd row. K2tog, knit to end…16 sts.
4th row. Purl to last 2 sts, P2tog…15 sts.
5th row. (K3, K2tog) 3 times…12 sts.
Place all sts from stitch-holders on needle and work 3 rows stocking st, beg with a purl row…30 sts.
Next row. (K3, K2tog) 6 times…24 sts.
Work 3 rows stocking st, beg with a purl row.
Next row. (K2, K2tog) 6 times…18 sts.
Work 3 rows stocking st, beg with a purl row.
Next row. (K2tog) 9 times…9 sts.
Cast off loosely.

NOSE

Using 3.00mm needles and C1, cast on 4 sts.
Work 6 rows stocking st (1st row is wrong side).
Cast off.
Work a gathering thread around outer edges and draw up tightly and fasten off securely.

EARS (make 4)

Using 3.00mm needles and M, cast on 13 sts.
Work 28 rows stocking st (1st row is wrong side).
Dec one st at beg of every row until 5 sts rem.
Cast off.

TAIL

Using 3.00mm needles and M, cast on 12 sts.
Work 16 rows stocking st (1st row is wrong side).
Cast off.
Work a gathering thread around outer edges and draw up tightly, filling firmly before fastening off securely.

To make up

With right sides tog, using a flat seam, and noting that purl side is right side of fabric, join Body pieces tog, leaving an opening at back. Stitch Head and Snout gusset tog, join the seam under the Head, leaving a 3cm opening at the back. Turn Head right side out. Stuff Head with filling. Join Head and Body using plastic joint pieces, as follows: place one half of joint into both Head and Body, pull up gathers around the joints and fasten off, then snap the joints tog, thus connecting the Head and Body. With right sides tog, join Ear pieces tog in pairs. Turn right side out, fold a pleat in the front of each Ear and stitch the Ears in place. With right sides tog, fold Legs and stitch seams, leaving an opening. With right sides tog, fold Arms and stitch seams, leaving an opening. Attach Arms and Legs to Body, using plastic joints, then stuff the limbs and Body with filling and stitch all openings. Attach Tail to back of Bunny. **Face:** Mark position of eyes. With a strong thread take a stitch through the Bunny's nose from the eye straight down to the chin, then back up to the second eye and down to the chin again, pulling the thread slightly to create an eye socket. Using brown stranded cotton and satin stitch (see **Embroidery Stitch Guide** on page 112), embroider eyes. Work a tiny dot of white in the centre of each eye for highlights. Attach Nose firmly to Bunny's snout as pictured. Blush cheeks lightly with red pencil.

PANTS

BACK (beg at first leg)

Using 4.00mm needles and C2, cast on 13 sts.
1st row. K2, *P1, K1, rep from * to last st, K1.
2nd row. K1, *P1, K1, rep from * to end.
3rd row. As 1st row, inc one st in centre...14 sts.
Work 3 rows stocking st, beg with a purl row.**
Leave rem sts on a stitch-holder.
Second Leg. Work as for First Leg to **.
Join Legs. Next row. Knit across 14 sts of second leg, then with right side facing, knit across 14 sts from left leg stitch-holder...28 sts.
Work 7 rows stocking st, beg with a purl row.
Next row. K13, cast off 2 sts (opening for tail), K13.
Next row. P13, *turn*, cast on 2 sts, *turn*, P13.
Work 8 rows stocking st, dec one st in centre...27 sts.
Waist. Change to 3.00mm needles.
Work 3 rows rib (as before).
Cast off in rib.

FRONT

Work as for Back, noting to omit cast off for tail.

BRACES (make 2)

**Using 4.00mm needles and C2, cast on 3 sts.
Knit in garter st until strap measures 2cm.**
Leave sts on a spare needle.
Rep from ** to **.
Next row. Knit across 3 sts from spare needle, then knit 3 sts on needle...6 sts.
Next row. K2tog, knit to last 2 sts, K2tog...4 sts.
Knit until work measures length desired.
Cast off.

To make up

Using backstitch, join side and inside leg seams of Pants.
Stitch Braces to front and back of Pants as pictured, crossing them at the back.

teddy BEAR

Every baby should have a teddy bear to love and, with his plump huggability, soft fur and endearing face, this little fellow is perfect.
Instructions begin overleaf.

Bear shown actual size.

Teddy Bear

Measurements

Finished bear is 25cm tall (18cm sitting).

Materials

- 50cm x 35cm mohair or synthetic fur fabric, pile length 5mm
- Fray preventative, such as Fray-Check
- One set of joints (Size 2): 25mm discs for head, 20mm for limbs
- One pair 7mm or 8mm snap-lock safety eyes
- Doll needle
- 7.5cm square felt or suede, for paws
- Brown Coton Perle 8 or stranded cotton, for nose
- Strong thread, for sewing
- Small bag polyester filling
- Ribbon for neck bow, optional

NOTE Fur fabrics, joints and safety eyes are all available from teddy bear and doll specialists or larger craft stores.

Pattern pieces

Pattern pieces are printed on pattern sheet in pink. Trace Side Head 57, Head Gusset 58, Muzzle 59, Ear 60, Side Front 61, Side Back 62, Outer Arm 63, Inner Arm 64, Paw Pad 65, Leg 66 and Foot Pad 67.

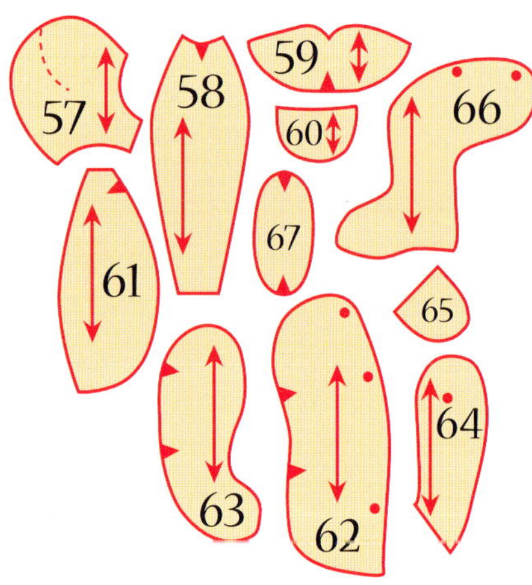

Cutting

NOTE 3.5mm seam allowance is **included** on all pieces. Stick traced pattern pieces onto thin cardboard or template plastic and carefully cut out pieces to make templates. Position the templates as shown in layout diagram, opposite, and draw around them using a fine line marker or pencil. Take care to reverse pattern pieces when required (as shown in layout diagram) and ensure that pile of fabric runs in the direction shown by grain lines on pattern pieces. Always use small sharp pointed scissors and cut very carefully, running the scissors under the pile and cutting the backing fabric only.

From fur fabric, cut two Side Heads, one Head Gusset, one Muzzle, four Ears, two Side Fronts, two Side Backs, two Outer Arms, two Inner Arms and four Legs.

From felt or suede, cut two Paw Pads (reversing pattern piece for second pad) and two Foot Pads.

Method

1 PREVENTING FRAYING Apply Fray-Check sparingly to the very edge of cut edges of fur fabric, to prevent fraying and stretching. Avoid applying it to the seamline. If fabric is very soft and has a tendency to fray, then apply Fray-Check to all cut edges before sewing. Firm backed fabrics only need to be treated where seams are left open for turning.

2 SEAMS Before seaming, pieces should be carefully oversewn together, by hand. As you work, use the needle to push the fur pile down between the two pieces to ensure well-covered seams. The final seaming can be done by hand, using neat small back stitch and strong thread, or by machine, stitching carefully along the seamline. Unless otherwise specified, all seams are stitched with right sides together.

3 HEAD Join Head Gusset to Side Heads, matching symbols. Matching point C on Muzzle to centre of Gusset, join seam D-C-D. Fold Muzzle in half and stitch from G to H. Turn head right side out and run a gathering thread around neck edge.

4 EYES Safety eyes should be inserted now, before head is stuffed. Position eyes at the point where Gusset seam joins Muzzle. Make tiny holes with the point of small sharp scissors, insert eye shanks into holes and snap the metal backing washer into place on the shank, pressing it on as firmly as possible.

5 HEAD JOINT Stuff head firmly. Insert neck joint into head, pull up gathering thread and tie off securely. (Joints can be fixed in various ways: usually cotter pins or lock nuts. Whichever one you choose, it is essential to make sure they are closed very firmly as they will loosen up once the bear is stuffed.)

joints into the limbs first, then pushing shank through into the body for locking. Use the point of small sharp scissors to make tiny holes, if necessary. Join head to body in the same way.

12 STUFFING Stuff limbs first, then body. Use a stuffing stick or blunt tool to pack stuffing down firmly, working carefully to shape and mould each piece to your satisfaction. Close openings with ladder stitch (see **Embroidery Stitch Guide**, on page 112). As long as strong thread is used, several stitches can be worked and then tightened really firmly to pull the two sides together securely and almost invisibly.

13 FINISHING Trim the Muzzle fur if desired and trim finished teddy with a neck bow.

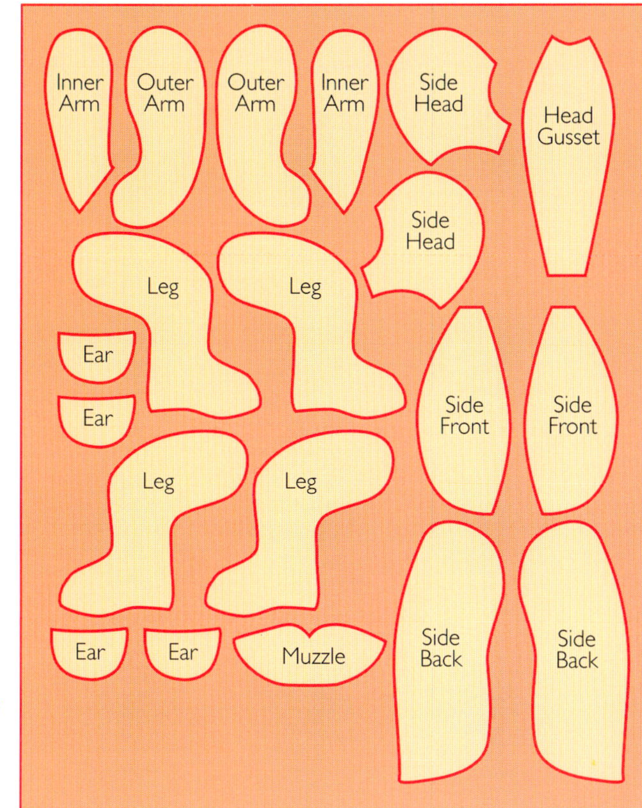

Layout of fur parts on piece 350mm x 500mm (half of a fat quarter)

6 EARS Sew Ears together in pairs around curved edge. Turn right side out. Sew Ears to head, turning under raw edges.

7 NOSE & MOUTH Clip fur pile from nose triangle area. Embroider the nose and mouth using two threads of brown cotton. Outline the nose area with a triangle of straight stitches, then fill in with close satin stitch, worked horizontally. Next, work a second row of vertical satin stitch over the first. Finally, outline the nose again with straight stitches and complete the mouth, as photographed.

8 LEGS Join Legs together in pairs, leaving opening in top edge, as indicated, and leaving foot edge open. With right sides together, stitch a Foot Pad to each Leg, matching leg seams to centre front and back of each Pad. Turn right side out.

9 ARMS Stitch a Paw Pad to lower end of each Inner Arm, then stitch Inner Arm to Outer Arm, leaving an opening for turning, as indicated. Turn right side out.

10 BODY Stitch centre front seam of Side Fronts, then stitch centre back seam of Side Backs, leaving opening as indicated. Stitch front to back at side seams and turn right side out through centre back opening.

11 JOINING LIMBS & HEAD TO BODY Join Arms and Legs to body as marked, inserting

ladybird LADYBIRD

With their jewel-like colours and reputation for bringing good luck, ladybirds make a delightful addition to a number of pretty and practical baby gifts – most of them wonderfully quick and simple to make as well.

An easy ladybird appliqué design can be used to embellish any number of purchased baby essentials, making them instantly a little more special. We used the design, which we have printed in three different sizes (see page 101 for more) to make a matching bath set of towel and face cloth. It also looks very sweet on a plain baby singlet and trainer pants, and could be used as well on all-in-one suits, a nappy (fold it first to ascertain where the motif should be placed) or bedlinen. To make the appliqué very easy, cut the body in one piece as well as the head section, use double-sided appliqué webbing to hold the pieces in place, then stitch around outline and add simple details using a close narrow zigzag.

If you don't feel confident about your drawing ability (although you really don't need much for tiny ladybirds), reduce the appliqué design on a photocopier until it is small enough to fit along a baby-sized wooden coathanger. Sand the hanger, give it a couple of coats of white acrylic paint, add a row of tiny red and black ladybirds, cover the hook with plastic tubing (from craft stores) and add matching ribbon trim. Very cute!

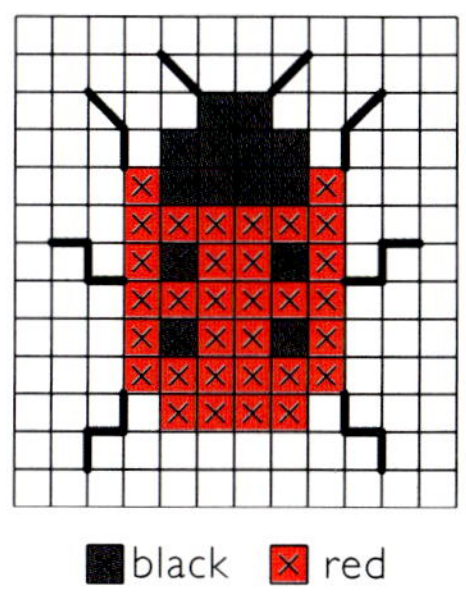

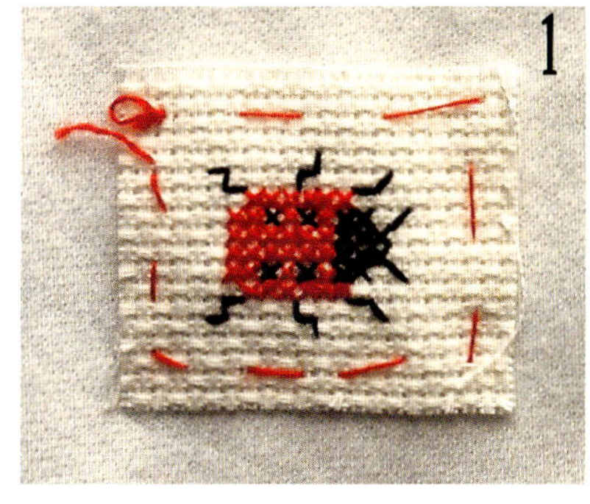

If you can do simple cross stitch, you can add embroidered ladybirds to just about anything. The trick to working cross stitch on finely woven fabric, such as this little T-shirt, is to use waste canvas, or a scrap of Aida. Baste a tiny rectangle of canvas or Aida to the spot where you want to work the motif, then, following the graph, above, work a ladybird, stitching through all layers (**Pic 1**). When design is finished, remove basting, then carefully pull the threads of canvas away, one by one, from beneath cross stitched design (**Pic 2**) until you're left with only the design. Of course, if you're working on even-weave fabric, such as the Aida cloth we used for the nursery hold-all, above, you can cross stitch directly onto the fabric itself. Instructions for the hold-all are on page 101.

cross my HEART

When time is short for producing a handmade gift for a new baby, this simple monogrammed heart sampler could be just what you're looking for. Quick to work in cross stitch, using two strands of embroidery cotton on Dublin linen (25-count), the colours can be varied as you choose – subtly different shades of a single colour, say blue, can also look very effective.

Cross Stitch Hearts Sampler

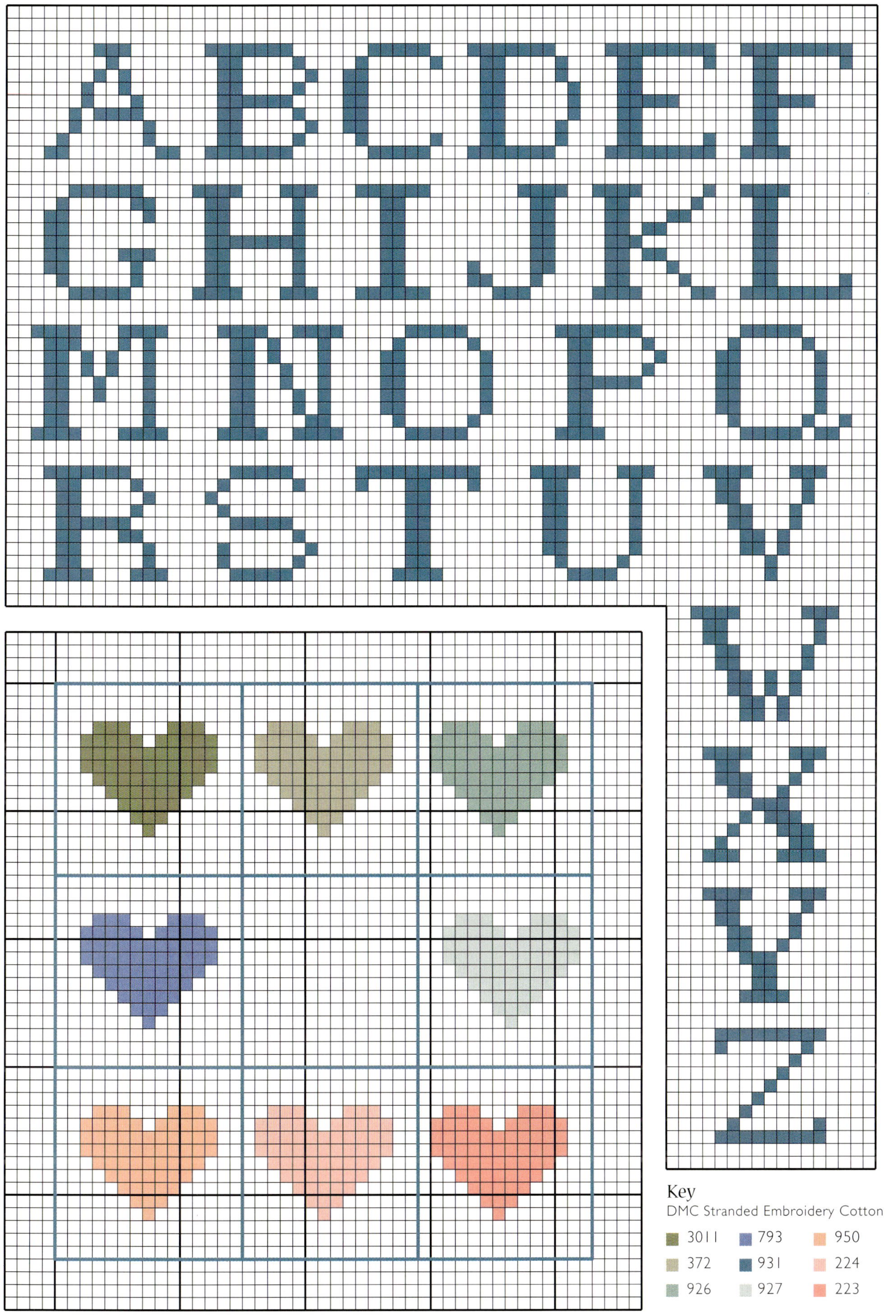

Key

DMC Stranded Embroidery Cotton

3011	793	950
372	931	224
926	927	223

make it QUICK

Sometimes, despite nine months' warning and the best of intentions, the Happy Event still catches us unprepared. There's no time now to whip up a complicated sampler or an heirloom shawl, but there is time to make one or more of the small gifts on the following pages, all of which have been designed with one thing in mind – speed.

Beautiful though they are, if you feel a bit daunted by the thought of creating a full-size heirloom birth sampler, why not try your hand at a miniature version instead? The tiny embroideries on these pages can be worked in a few hours and the effect is charming. Using letters and motifs from the heart sampler on page 61, the decorative alphabets and borders on pages 116 and 117, or from your own favourite cross stitch alphabet, work single initials and designs on scraps of cream Dublin linen or 14-count Aida, using two strands of thread. Frame your work in miniature unfinished pine frames – Ikea does a very inexpensive set of five – or paint a craftwood frame in a colour to match your design. For a quick and unusual keepsake birth "sampler", work a single initial for one frame, a tiny embroidered heart or flower for the second, and baby's birth date for the third. Stitch the framed embroideries to a length of satin or grosgrain ribbon so that they can be displayed together.

24.12.
2000
MIA

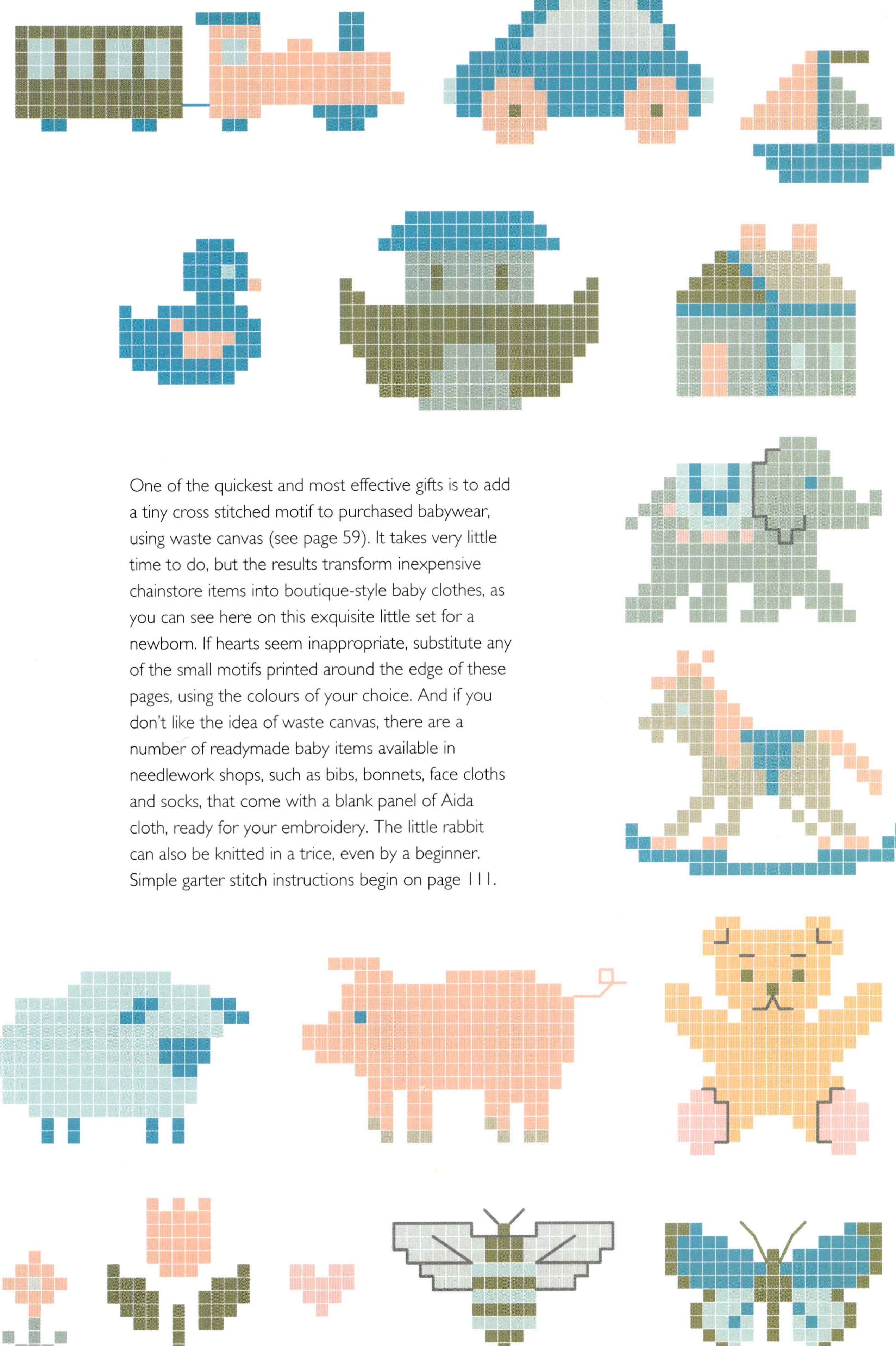

One of the quickest and most effective gifts is to add a tiny cross stitched motif to purchased babywear, using waste canvas (see page 59). It takes very little time to do, but the results transform inexpensive chainstore items into boutique-style baby clothes, as you can see here on this exquisite little set for a newborn. If hearts seem inappropriate, substitute any of the small motifs printed around the edge of these pages, using the colours of your choice. And if you don't like the idea of waste canvas, there are a number of readymade baby items available in needlework shops, such as bibs, bonnets, face cloths and socks, that come with a blank panel of Aida cloth, ready for your embroidery. The little rabbit can also be knitted in a trice, even by a beginner. Simple garter stitch instructions begin on page 111.

Fluffy pompoms are available in a variety of colours and sizes from craft stores and can be used to make all sorts of delightful – and quick – baby gifts. The bunny cards at left, for instance, can be made in minutes. Using a glue gun (not essential, but it does make the job much easier) glue a smaller sized pompom head to a larger pompom body, then glue a tiny pompom muzzle to the front of the head. When joining pompoms, simply part the fibres of the larger pompom, add a spot of glue and press the smaller pompom into position. Add glass bead eyes, nylon thread whiskers and facial features with a fine black pen. Construct ears from felt scraps, as pictured, then glue ears to a readymade frame card (available from craft and needlework shops) and glue the pompom rabbit in place on the card.

Pompoms can also be used to create delightful mobiles for the nursery. To make the fluffy ducklings on this page, glue two yellow pompoms (28mm and 55mm) together, cutting off the top of the larger ball first to create the duckling's flat back. Trim tails to a pointed shape with scissors, then add orange felt beaks and feet, and black seed beads for eyes. Using nylon thread or fine black cotton, hang ducklings from two painted wooden baby-sized coathangers, screwed together at right angles with the metal hook. Decorate with wooden beads as desired and hang well out of baby's reach.

The fluffly little handfuls of heaven, opposite below, can also be used to make a mobile or, in a smaller size, to decorate a card. For each mobile-sized teddy bear you need pompoms as follows: 1 x 50mm for body, 1 x 38mm for head, 6 x 25mm for legs and upper arms, 5 x 20mm for paws, ears and muzzle, and 1 x 6mm (black) for nose. Join pompoms to each other, cutting away about one third on each ear pompom to flatten the front, before gluing. Add black seed bead eyes and a narrow neck ribbon, if desired. Remember, these toys are *not* for small children or babies to handle.

Soft, colourful building blocks make an eye-catching quick gift. If you have access to a foam rubber shop, get them to cut foam cubes in the sizes of your choice. Otherwise, cut and glue car washing sponges into a cube. From brightly coloured felt, cut six squares 5mm larger than one side of your cube. Cut six appliqué shapes from felt scraps (using the appliqué outlines on the pattern sheet, enlarging/reducing as needed) and glue one to each felt square with craft glue, making sure edges are firmly glued. With contrast embroidery thread (we used Perle Coton 5), oversew squares together, joining sides first, then adding top before inserting foam cube and adding bottom. To make the block into a rattle, cut a hollow in the centre of the foam and add a little bell, before covering, if desired.

Standard white singlets and nappies are much less boring with the addition of a simple appliqué motif. Using the outlines on the pattern sheet and following the **Basic Appliqué Techniques** on page 118, these cheerful garments were created in a flash – for very little cash.

pretty in PINK

What sweeter way to welcome a special baby girl to the world than with this celebratory garland of cross stitched hearts? For a complete nursery theme, the motifs can also be used to decorate other items, such as a pretty gingham cot quilt, or added to Aida band to turn plain purchased bedlinen into a matching set for a tiny occupant.

Good Night
Sleep Tight

Garland of Hearts

Measurements

***Large heart** measures 14cm x 15cm.*
***Medium heart** measures 11cm x 14cm.*
***Small heart** measures 7.5cm x 9cm.*

Materials

- 0.25m x 160cm Permin pink check evenweave cotton fabric, 9 threads/cm, for embroidery and backing (see NOTE, below)
- 3.2m x 3mm satin ribbon in *each* of pink and white
- One skein DMC Stranded Embroidery Cotton in each of the following colours: dk lavender 209, med. lavender 210, coral 351, pale yellow 744, cardinal red 3801, lt fuchsia 3806, teal blue 3810, ice blue 3811, lime 3819 and tangerine 3825
- 100g polyester fibrefill
- Size 24 or 26 tapestry needle
- Machine thread

NOTE Permin embroidery fabric is available from specialist needlework shops. If pastel check is not available, use plain pale pink or cream.

Small Heart Graph

Method

1 CROSS STITCH Zigzag or overlock edges of fabric to prevent fraying. Following the graph and colour key on the pattern sheet, work cross stitch (see **Embroidery Stitch Guide** on page 112), using two strands of cotton over two threads of fabric. Work the central column of motifs of the large heart design first, beginning the top motif approximately 4cm from the selvedge of the fabric. Then work two of the medium hearts next to the large heart, leaving approximately 4cm between each. Work one small heart on the remaining space on each side of the medium hearts, leaving 2cm on the side edges and 3cm between each heart.

2 MAKING UP HEARTS Cut carefully around each heart, leaving 1cm seam allowance. From leftover Permin fabric, cut a rectangular backing piece for each heart, at least 1cm larger than the outer edges of the heart. Match checks if possible. Cut pink and white ribbon into 30cm lengths and sort into sets of pink/white pairs.

With raw edges even, right sides together, and using the photograph as a guide to positioning, pin then baste a pink/white ribbon pair to the rounded top on both sides of each cross stitched heart. With right sides together, pin embroidered heart and backing piece together, sandwiching raw ends of ribbon pairs in between. With wrong side of cross stitch facing you so that outline of heart can be used as a guide, stitch around heart, leaving a small opening on one side for turning, taking care not to catch ribbon ends in seam. Trim excess backing and seam allowance close to seam, clip top indentation and curves and turn heart right side out. Fill each heart with fibrefill and slipstitch opening closed.

Tie hearts together with bows to form cot string.

Key

DMC Stranded Embroidery Cotton

Symbol	DMC	Symbol	DMC
•	209	●	3806
✱	210	◥	3810
▲	351	L	3811
X	744	O	3819
■	3801	S	3825

Gingham Cot Quilt

Finished quilt measures approximately 105cm x 75cm.

Materials

- 2m x 115cm pink gingham, 8 squares/inch
- 1.2m x 80cm thin wadding
- One skein DMC Stranded Embroidery Cotton in each of the colours listed under **Garland of Hearts**, opposite
- Size 24 or 26 tapestry needle
- Embroidery hoop
- Machine thread

Method

1 CUTTING From gingham, cut two rectangles, each 107cm x 77cm, and eight strips, each 50cm x 4.5cm, for Ties. From wadding, cut one rectangle, 107cm x 77cm. 1cm seam allowance is included in measurements.

2 CROSS STITCH Place one piece of gingham in embroidery hoop, with the working area of the fabric centred and the top of the hoop approximately 25cm below the top edge of the fabric. Working with a hoop will help to keep stitches evenly tensioned despite the fineness of the gingham.

Following graph and colour key on pattern sheet, and using two strands of thread over one gingham square, cross stitch the Medium Heart in the centre of the fabric, starting with the central column of small pink hearts. When stitching is complete, press on wrong side on a well-padded surface.

3 TIES Fold each Tie in half lengthwise, right sides together, and stitch long edge and across one short edge. Turn right side out and press. With right sides together and raw edges even, pin four pairs of Ties along lower edge of embroidered quilt top, positioning two outer pairs approximately 15cm in from each end; place remaining two pairs evenly between the first two. Baste to hold.

4 ASSEMBLING QUILT Place embroidered quilt top, with right side uppermost, on a flat surface, keeping Ties out of the way of the seam. Centre quilt back on top of front, with right sides together. Lay wadding on top of quilt back, smoothing out any wrinkles. Starting from the centre and working out towards the edges, baste all three layers together. Trim wadding if necessary, then stitch around edges, leaving a 15cm opening on one long side for turning. Trim the seam allowances and turn quilt right side out. Press under raw edges of opening, then slipstitch opening closed.

5 FINISHING Using two strands of 744 embroidery thread, work a row of running stitch 1cm in from quilt edges. To "tie" layers together, work random single cross stitches all over quilt using two strands of 744, tying ends of cotton together at the back. Remove basting. Quilt can be kept in place by tying it firmly to lower rungs of cot.

To embellish purchased Aida band for bedlinen and towels, adapt repeat patterns from the cross stitch hearts, and add a bedtime message (see pattern sheet) in the centre of the band, if desired.

welcome!

An embroidered birth sampler, recording a baby's name and birth date is a traditional and very special gift for a newborn. Based on the age-old format of a band sampler and incorporating a number of traditional motifs, this beautiful piece uses subtly variegated shades of hand-dyed silks in cross stitch and satin stitch to capture that softly faded look of a precious heirloom sampler.

Rebecca's Sampler

Measurements

Finished design measures 35cm x 8.5cm.

Materials

- 25cm x 45cm Zweigart "Belfast" écru linen (32-count)
- One skein Gumnut "Stars" Hand-dyed Silk in each of the following colours: lt grey-green 626, med. grey-green 628, v. lt fern green 677, fern green 647, v. lt beige-brown 947, med. beige-brown 949, lt salmon 823 and dk salmon 857

Or

- One skein DMC Stranded Embroidery Cotton in each of the following colours: lt grey-green 927, med. grey-green 926, dk grey-green 3768, v. lt fern green 524, fern green 522, v. lt beige-brown 842, med. beige-brown 840, lt salmon 760 and dk salmon 3328 (see NOTE, below)
- Size 26 tapestry needle

NOTE Gumnut yarns (www.gumnutyarns.com/) are available from specialist needlework shops. If you are using DMC threads, the results, although charming, will differ slightly from the photograph. Hand-dyed silks produce slight variations in tone that stranded cotton cannot achieve. A more traditional look can be obtained by "tweeding" some shades of cotton in some areas. Use one strand *each* of 760 and 3328 for a blended effect in the second row of fruit in the basket and on the large trees; use one strand *each* of 926 and 3768 in the house and the birds.

Method

1 PREPARATION The graph for the sampler is printed on the pattern sheet. Before starting to stitch, pencil in desired lettering from alphabet provided opposite, onto the blank spaces on the graph. Allow one space between letters and three spaces between words, although these spaces can be altered in order to fit words into one line, if preferred. We have allowed three lines for the name and two lines for the date, but because this design has no borders, extra lettering may be added. The material size given also allows up to three additional lines – just remember to adjust the centre lines to accommodate them.

2 EMBROIDERY Following the graph on the pattern sheet and the **Embroidery Stitch Guide** on page 112, work cross stitch using two strands of silk or cotton over two threads of linen. Work satin stitch as follows: top row, two strands very light beige-brown over four threads of linen; second row, two strands very light fern green over four threads of linen; strawberries in alphabet, two strands light salmon over varying lengths according to graph; bottom three rows, two strands very light fern green over varying lengths according to graph. Work letters in light grey-green.

3 FINISHING When all embroidery is complete, press linen on the back on a well-padded surface and frame as desired.

it's a BOY!

If the pastel hearts and flowers of traditional birth samplers seem inappropriate to welcome a bouncing baby boy, this unusual canvaswork lion might prove the perfect gift. Inspired by a 16th century textile pattern, the tapestry makes an ideal present for a little boy and can still be affectionately displayed when he has long outgrown teddy bears and tank engines. The tapestry can of course be framed, but it could also be mounted in a cushion or, as we show here, used to personalise a very beautiful photograph album.

ALEXANDER
SEPTEMBER 18 1995

Alexander's Lion

Measurements

Finished design measures 15cm square.

Materials

- 30cm square mono-point canvas, 18-count
- DMC Perle Coton No 5 in the following colours and amounts: three skeins dark green 890, one skein *each* red 304, blue 930, light green 503, straw yellow 676, medium gold 729, dull gold 680 and metallic gold
- Size 22 tapestry needle
- Canvaswork frame (optional)

Method

1 PREPARATION Place canvas into frame, if using. It is not necessary to use a frame, but doing so will reduce the amount of distortion of the canvas as you work tent stitch.

2 EMBROIDERY Using the alphabet graph on page 83, work out your own personal lettering and date. Following the design graph, opposite, and the **Embroidery Stitch Guide** on page 112, work the design in tent stitch, using one strand of perle coton over one thread of canvas. Work the background in basketweave stitch in dark green 890.

3 FINISHING When all embroidery is complete, remove canvas from frame. If it is very distorted, it will need to be "blocked", that is, stretched back to shape by gently damping and pinning into the correct shape on a board, until dry. If you are not confident about doing this, many specialist needlework shops will do it for you. The work can then be framed, or used as desired – see instructions for photograph album on page 82.

Key DMC Perle Coton No 5

304 · 930 · 503 · 676 · 729 · 680 · metallic gold

Handmade Photograph Album

Measurements

Approximately 30.5cm square.

Materials

- Two pieces heavyweight cardboard, each 305mm x305mm (see NOTE, below)
- Craft knife and ruler
- 0.4m x 90cm thin batting
- Spray adhesive
- 0.4m x 115cm fabric to coordinate with cross stitch
- 450 adhesive
- Tapestry panel (see page 80)
- Double-sided tape
- 0.7m coordinating narrow cord with flange, or readymade piping
- One piece coloured paper or thin board, to line inside cover
- Heavyweight black paper for pages (we used acid-free paper, pre-cut to A3, 420mm x 297mm)
- Acid-free tissue paper or lightweight tracing paper for interleaves (A3, if possible)
- One piece gold tissue paper, for flyleaf, if desired
- Three brass album connectors
- 1.3m tasselled cord, if desired

NOTE All the archival-quality cardboard and paper can be purchased from artists' supplies stores or specialist paper shops.

Method

1 WINDOW FRAME In the centre of one piece of heavyweight board, measure and rule a square the same size as the finished measurements of your tapestry. Carefully cut out window with a craft knife. Rule a margin 35mm in from one side of the board and score with craft knife.

2 PADDING Using a sparing amount of spray adhesive, cover the *unscored* side of board with thin batting, cutting away batting to fit around edges and window. Cover one side of remaining uncut board with batting in the same way.

3 FABRIC COVER Cut two pieces of fabric, each approximately 335mm square, and lay them face down on your work surface. Place back cover (uncut piece), batting side down, onto the centre of one fabric square. Turn edges of fabric over and glue to wrong side of board, using 450 adhesive – top and bottom first, then sides. Fold in corners to neaten. Repeat with front cover, snipping diagonally into corners of window frame and folding fabric back around board to inside.

Glue flanged cord or piping around inside of window so that cord just extends beyond frame. Place tapestry face down in window and tape in position. (Make sure your cover is the right way up: when you look at the cover from the front, the scored margin should be on the left (on the inside) to allow the cover to open.)

4 COVER LINING Cut two pieces of coloured paper slightly smaller than covers. Use glue or double-sided tape to attach to inside covers, concealing raw edges of fabric cover. You may have to slit the lining paper on the inside front cover where it has been scored, to allow the cover to fold back.

5 PAGES Cut black pages to measure 297mm (side) x 327mm (top). Rule a margin 30mm in from side edge on each page, score along this line and fold the margin inwards onto the page to give a square page with a reinforced margin. Use a little double-sided tape to glue the margins down. Cut tissue or tracing paper into 297mm squares. Use a little double-sided tape to attach a tissue sheet to each black page along the margin. Stack pages together.

Cut two sheets of gold tissue paper, each 297mm square. Attach one at the front and one at the back of the stack of pages.

6 SPINE Cut a piece of coloured lining paper, 297mm x 75mm. Using spray adhesive, glue this strip to a spare scrap of cover fabric and trim edges of fabric even with paper.

7 ASSEMBLING ALBUM Place page stack between covers. (Cover should be slightly larger.) Fold the fabric-covered spine around the lefthand edge of the pages and tuck the ends in beneath the covers.

Mark three evenly-spaced holes in cover using a pencil or fine marker. You can make your own holes through all layers, using an awl or even an electric drill, but we found it much easier to take our album to the local printer and have him drill the holes for us. Connect the album together with the brass connector screws.

8 FINISHING A gold tasselled cord can be tied around the front cover and knotted for a special finish.

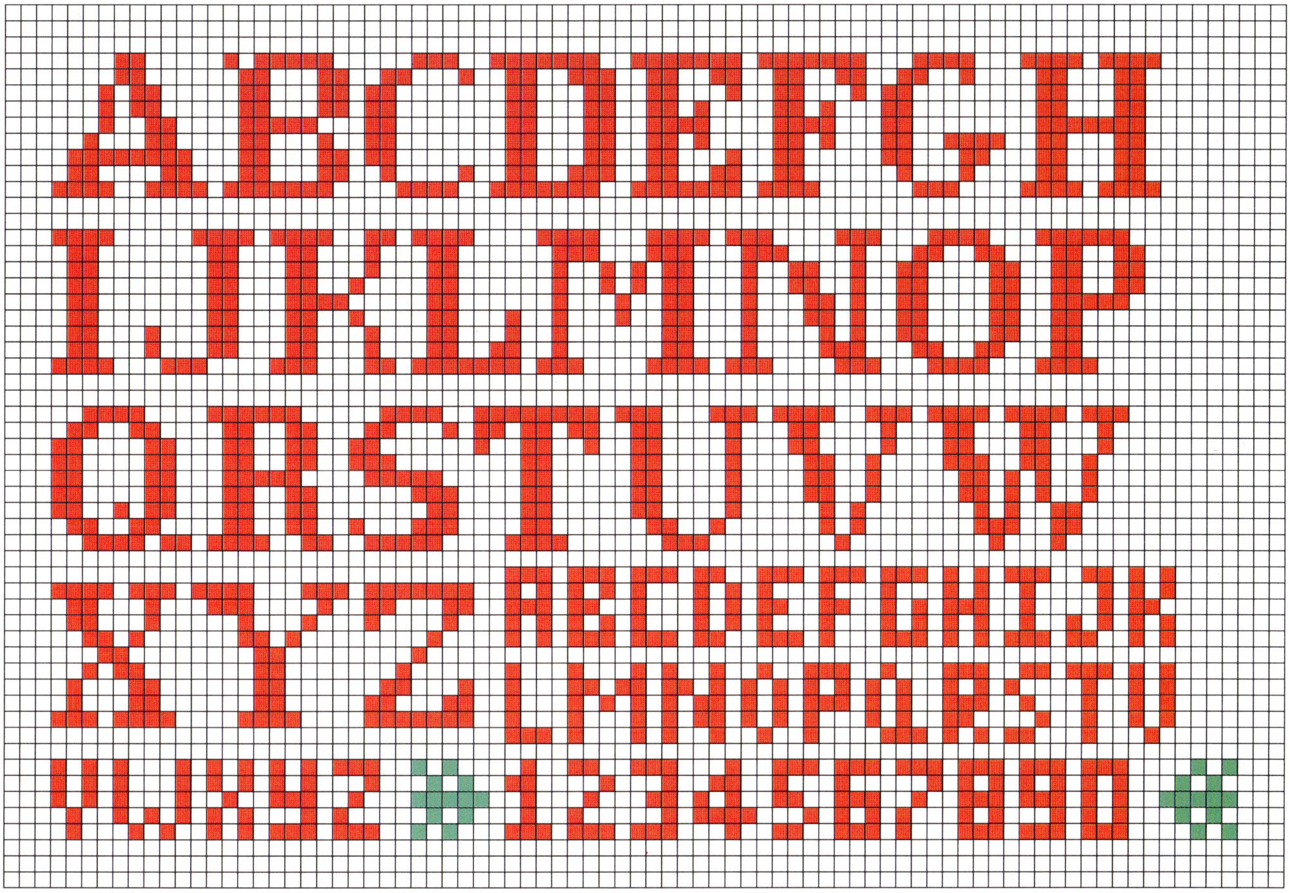
ABCDEFGH
IJKLMNOP
QRSTUVW
XYZ ABCDEFGHIJK
LMNOPQRSTU
VWXYZ 1234567890

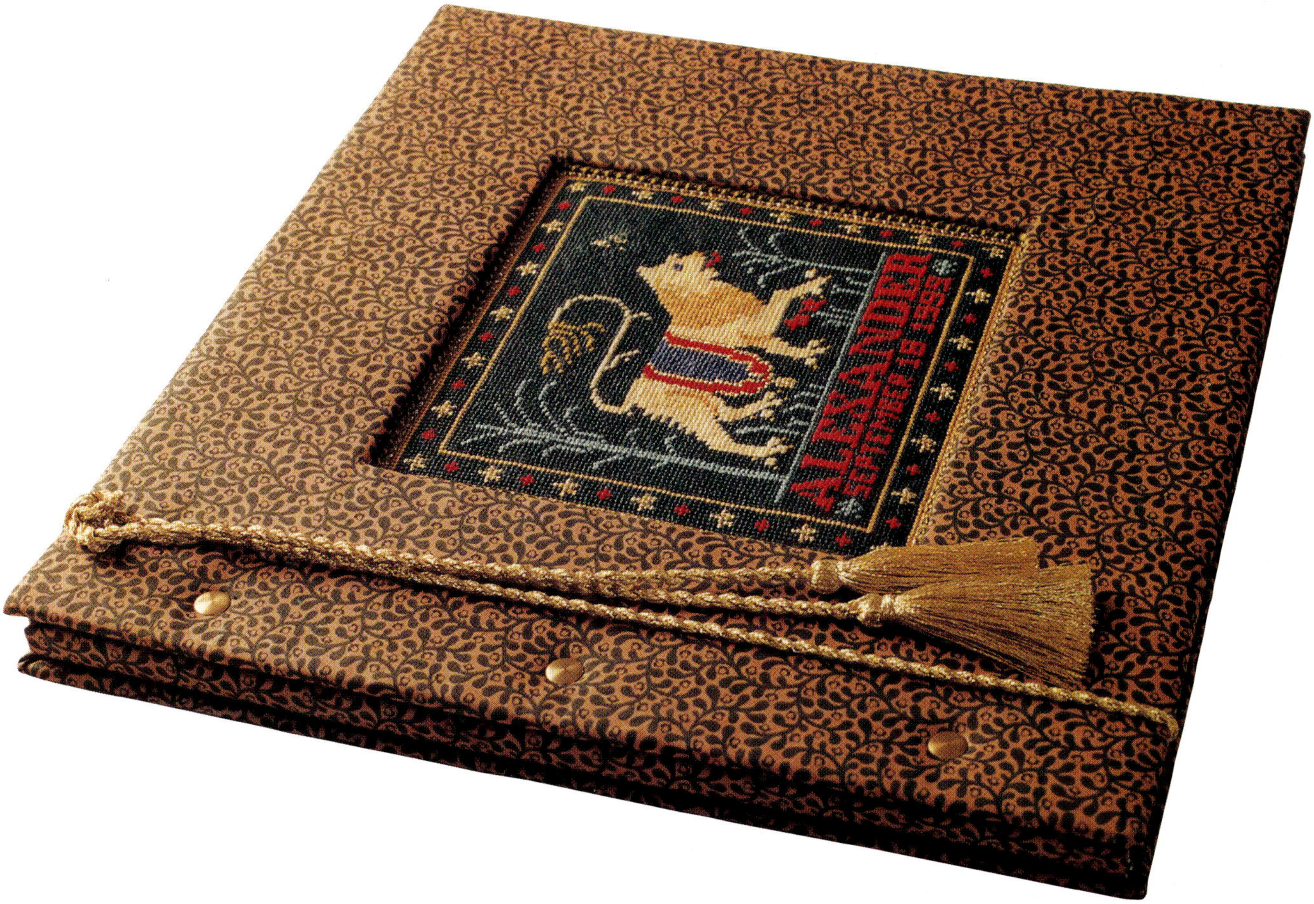
ALEXANDER

snug as a BUG

This exquisite baby blanket, although intricate-looking, is really not difficult – it only uses four simple stitches. Once you've worked the ribbon outline, the flowers can be placed as you choose, rather than following a rigid design. But if the blanket seems too big a project, why not start with the pretty matching monogrammed pincushion, a beautiful little gift in itself.

Wool-Embroidered Baby Blanket

Measurements

Our blanket is approximately 110cm x 80cm, to fit a bassinet, but the design can be adapted to any sized blanket.

Materials

- Bassinet-sized pure wool blanketing, 110cm x 80cm
- Thin tracing paper
- Dark sewing thread
- One skein each embroidery wool in the following brands and colours (or substitute your own choice): **Paterna** A701 deep gold, A711 light gold, A756 cream, A514 light grey-blue, A704 buttermilk, A727 yellow, A923 dusty rose, A652 green, A653 light green; **DMC Medici** 8120A mushroom pink, 8123 burgundy, 8026 yellow, 8309 deep brown-green, 8405 green, 8331 lilac, 8176 rust; **Appletons** 603 light grape, 604 grape, 292 moss green
- Paterna Embroidery Wool: two skeins A504 smoke blue
- DMC light gold thread (Art 282), or similar
- Crewel embroidery needle
- 122cm x 92cm cotton fabric, for backing
- DMC Coton Perle No 5: three skeins colour 332

Method

1 PREPARATION Fold blanketing in half widthwise and lengthwise to find centre. Full-sized design for embroidery is printed on pattern sheet. Trace circle from design onto tracing paper, cut out, leaving a 1cm border all around, and place on back of blanketing,

placing centre of circle directly in centre of fabric, or slightly below centre, depending on preference. Pin circle in place, tack around outline with a dark sewing thread, then tear paper carefully away. Alternatively, trace circle onto fabric with a light pencil, remove pattern and tack around outline.

2 TRACING RIBBON PATTERN Getting the ribbon pattern in position is probably the most difficult part of the whole project. Spend a little time getting it right, as it sets the framework for the whole piece. No other flowers are marked on the blanket. This allows you complete freedom to fill the spaces, using the design as a guide.

Trace bow and ribbon pieces from design onto tracing paper. Cut out, turn over, and place in position on back of fabric, over tacked circle. (Because you are working on the back of the fabric, you must work in mirror image so things will be the right way round on the front.) A quick tracing of circle, bow and ribbons taken from the design and flipped over gives a good guide to positioning your pieces.

Trace lightly around pattern pieces and tack over tracing line in dark thread to mark pattern outline clearly. Turn blanket to right side and you'll have a perfect outline of circle, ribbon and bow.

3 EMBROIDERY Start your embroidery by practising a few stitches on a scrap of fabric, following the **Wool Embroidery Guide** on page 115. The ribbon and bow should be embroidered first, as many of the flowers overlap them. Bow and ribbons are worked in satin stitch, using smoke blue. The ribbon is outlined in stem stitch, using gold thread.

To start the flowers, embroider three or four large daisies in a section. Daisies are made up of a number of lazy daisy stitches, filled with straight stitches of a different colour. Try using Paterna yarns in different combinations, such as buttermilk filled with straight stitches of cream; light gold filled with yellow. Slightly smaller daisies have been embroidered in clusters, using deep gold filled with light gold. Other small daisies have been stitched in cream lazy daisy stitch, but not filled with straight stitch. All centres of daisies are French knots. To fill larger daisies, four or five knots should be used, whereas smaller daisies will need between one and three. Choose a centre to match flower, such as deep brown-green to add a dark centre to the stronger daisies, gold for lighter large daisies and yellow (Paterna A727) for smaller cream daisies.

Add leaves of lazy daisy stitches around flowers. Green (Paterna A652) is good for darker daisies, and light green (Paterna A653) for cream daisies.

Embroider lavender using lazy daisy stitches in a fish-bone pattern, referring to design for approximate positioning. Curve the stitches as you work, to make lavender look more natural. Use two different threads at once, such as light grape and grape, to give a greater depth of colour. Stems are worked in stem stitch, using moss green. Random straight stitches of moss green should also be added along the lavender flower for interest.

Now you can fill the remaining area to your heart's delight! Add flurries of forget-me-nots in smoke blue and light grey-blue, working five blue French knots with a centre French knot in yellow (DMC Medici 8026). Add small lazy daisy stitches randomly in green (DMC Medici 8405).

Add clusters of winter roses, working three lazy daisy stitches from the same point downwards, using mushroom pink. Two leaves are added in lazy daisy stitch, from the same starting point, but pointing upwards in green (DMC Medici 8405). Extra leaves should also be added randomly.

Fill remaining spaces with little flowers, worked with five lazy daisy stitches, in colours of your choice, such as lilac, dusty rose or yellow. Tiny five-pointed flowers worked in burgundy also add depth and interest. Other five-pointed flowers of deep gold can be filled with straight stitches of rust.

Some flowers should overlap the ribbon, to give a more natural look, as though the ribbon were weaving through the flowers. Use the circle as a guide and keep approximately equidistant either side of the tacked line. When you are happy with the effect, repeat your work in different sections, but do not try to repeat exactly. For example, instead of four daisies, you may have only three, and more small cream daisies. Make slightly different combinations; add flurries of forget-me-nots in different areas. Stop every now and then to look at your work. You will see what it needs.

When you are happy with the final piece, fill any spaces with flowers to balance the circle. Add French knots randomly throughout the design, in DMC gold thread and DMC Coton Perle, to add lustre. Pull out tacking thread.

4 ASSEMBLING BLANKET To assemble, place backing fabric, right side down on floor, centre blanket, right side up, on top. Fold under 1cm on edges of backing fabric, then fold again to form a 5cm binding, and pin in place. Slipstitch folded edge of binding to blanketing, sewing right through both layers to catch backing fabric, and mitring corners for neatness.

5 TWISTED CORD Take six strands of Coton Perle and two strands of gold thread, each measuring 2.5m. Knot each end of the bundle and, either get someone to hold one end, or fix it to a door, window or chair. Stretch threads and twist until you feel a resistance, then, without slacking the threads, find the middle point and allow cords to twist back on one another from this middle point, forming a thick cord. Make two cords of this length for the two longer sides of blanket, and repeat process for shorter sides, starting with two bundles of 2m threads. Finish blanket with a twisted cord, stitched to the front of blanket, along inner edge of binding. Alternatively, you could use piping, purchased or homemade, and secure it when stitching binding in place.

To neaten ends when sewing cord to blanket, tuck them into corners or make small loops at each corner.

Pincushion

Measurements

Approximately 14cm square.

Materials

- Two squares wool blanketing, each 16cm x 16cm
- Thin tracing paper
- Dark sewing thread
- One skein embroidery wool in each of the following brands and colours (or substitute your own choice): **Paterna** A504 smoke blue, A701 deep gold, A711 light gold; **DMC Medici** 8309 deep brown-green, 8120A mushroom pink, 8123 burgundy, 8026 yellow, 8405 green, 8331 lilac, 8716 rust
- DMC light gold thread (Art 282)
- DMC Coton Perle No 5, colour 332
- Crewel embroidery needle
- A few tiny gold seed beads, optional
- Old stockings or sawdust, to fill

Method

1 PREPARATION Fold one blanketing square in half widthwise and lengthwise to find centre point. Full-size design for embroidery is printed on pattern sheet. Trace circle and square from design onto tracing paper. Cut out square and centre on back of blanketing square. Tack outline in dark thread, as for Embroidered Blanket, **Step 1**, page 86. Do the same for the circle. Do not trace any flowers onto blanketing: design should be used as a guide only.

2 EMBROIDERY On front of blanketing, work large daisies first, using deep gold lazy daisy stitch, filled in with straight stitches of light gold (see **Wool Embroidery Guide** on page 115). Work centres using four French knots of deep brown-green. A fly stitch of rust can also be worked at the point of each petal. Add buds, using lazy daisy stitch in deep gold. Add leaves in green.

Work smaller five-pointed daisies in deep gold lazy daisy stitch; fill with rust straight stitches.

Forget-me-nots are worked in French knots, using smoke blue with yellow centres.

Add more five-pointed flowers in yellow, lilac and mushroom pink, scattering green leaves randomly throughout. Keep approximately within the pattern lines to achieve the shaped effect.

Gold beads can be added randomly if desired, or make French knots with gold thread. French knots of Coton Perle are also added for lustre.

3 MONOGRAM Using the alphabet, on these pages, trace desired initial onto thin tracing paper. Pin to right side of blanketing and tack through paper along marked lines. Tear away paper and fill work initial using satin stitch in smoke blue.

4 BACKING SQUARE A few random flowers may be stitched in the centre of the remaining blanketing square as a pretty touch for the back of the pincushion.

To assemble cushion, place blanketing squares right sides together. Allowing a 1cm seam, machine-stitch along edges, leaving a small opening. Clip corners and turn right side out. Fill with old stockings or sawdust. Slipstitch opening closed.

5 FINISHING Make a twisted cord as for Embroidered Blanket, **Step 5**, page 87, using threads two and a half times the desired finished length. Slipstitch cord to edge of pincushion, attaching a tassel at one corner, if desired (see **Step 6**, below) and allowing some excess cord at one corner to form a loop.

6 TASSEL Wind Coton Perle and gold thread (approximately 50 times per tassel) around a small rectangle of cardboard (width of cardboard equals approximate length of tassel). Slip a length of thread under wound threads to secure tassel at top. Cut threads at bottom to release tassel from cardboard and wind approximately 30cm gold thread around tassel near top, to form neck.

twinkle TWINKLE

Add a touch of heaven to baby's bedtime with this wonderfully soft polar fleece cot blanket and matching slippers. The celestial blue double-sided blanket is dotted with stars – both appliquéd and embroidered – and finished with simple blanket stitch edging. The little slippers, each sporting a smaller sized star, have dots of dimensional paint applied to their soles to make them non-slip.

Polar Fleece Baby Blanket and Slippers

Measurements

Blanket measures 90cm x 120cm.
Slippers to fit a baby up to 12 months (foot length approximately 13cm).

Materials

- 1.5m x 150cm-wide polar fleece in both blue and white
- Sewing and basting thread
- DMC Soft Cotton (Retors Mat, Art 89): 1 skein blue (to match blue polar fleece) and 5 skeins white
- DMC Stranded Metallic Embroidery Thread: 1 skein silver
- Dimensional fabric paint: white

Method

BLANKET

1 CUTTING From polar fleece, cut one blue rectangle and one white rectangle, each 90cm x 120cm. From scraps, cut six white Stars, using the larger of the outlines on the pattern sheet (in pink).

2 APPLIQUÉ Divide the blue rectangle into a grid of 30cm squares (12 squares in all), using large basting stitches. Appliqué a star onto every alternate square by working small overcasting stitches around the edge, using white machine thread. Using the photograph as a guide, embroider a simple centre motif on each appliquéd star, using blue embroidery thread.

3 EMBROIDERY In each of the empty squares, work simple snowflakes in straight stitches, using silver and white embroidery thread, as photographed.

4 JOINING LAYERS When embroidery is complete, place the blue and white rectangles together, with wrong sides together. Secure the two layers to each other by stitching close to the basted grid lines. Remove the basting.

5 BINDING Bind outer edges together using blanket stitch (see **Embroidery Stitch Guide** on page 112) in white embroidery thread, spacing the stitches about 1cm apart.

SLIPPERS

1 CUTTING Pattern pieces are printed on the pattern sheet in a pink tone. Trace Sole, Front and Heel. From blue polar fleece, cut two Soles, four Fronts and four Heels. From white polar fleece, cut two Stars, using the smaller Star outline, printed above.

2 JOINING UPPER SECTIONS All the seams are worked by hand in small overcasting stitches, using white embroidery thread and placing the wrong sides of the fabric together. For each slipper, stitch two Heel pieces together along centre back seam (B), and two Fronts together along centre front seam (C). Next, stitch completed sections together at each side (D).

3 SOLES Stitch the Sole into place on each completed slipper upper.

4 FINISHING Work a line of overcasting around the upper edge of each slipper and stitch a white star to the front of each.

5 NON-SLIP SURFACE Using the photograph as a guide, cover the bottom of each Sole completely with small dots of white dimensional paint and allow to dry for 24 hours. These dots will help to prevent the fabric from slipping on shiny floors. (After 72 hours, the paint will have cured enough to be washable.)

easy as ABC

Nothing beats the snuggly softness of pure wool for keeping baby warm. This wonderful little cot blanket features a feather-stitched grid and naïve country-style motifs, worked in simple colourful cross stitch on a traditional cream background. With its soft cotton backing, the blanket would also make a comfortable floor rug for a spot of gentle leg kicking.

Cross Stitched Cot Blanket

Measurements

Finished blanket measures 78cm x 110cm.

Materials

- 80cm x 120cm off-white pure wool cot blanket or blanketing
- Appletons Crewel Wool in the following colours and quantities: seven skeins 504; one skein each 321, 324, 754, 756, 764, 843 and 982
- Fifteen 14cm x 16cm pieces linen 10 (10 threads per cm or 25 threads per inch), see NOTE, below
- 0.8m x 120cm cream cotton fabric, for backing
- Size 24 chenille needle
- Tacking thread
- Cream machine thread
- Ruler, tape measure and pins

NOTE The colour of the linen you use does not matter as it will be pulled away from beneath the stitching, so scraps of different colours can be used, as long as the thread count is the same. You could also use any other 25-count even-weave fabric, such as Lugana. Waste canvas, although cheapest, is not really suitable for this job, as it does not sit nicely on the blanketing and tends to damage the pile.

Method

1 PREPARATION Tack a frame around the outside of the blanketing, 2.5cm from the outside edge. Inside the frame, tack a grid of lines that divides the blanket equally into five divisions across and six down.

2 FEATHER STITCH GRID Using Appletons 504, work a row of feather stitch (see **Embroidery Stitch Guide** on page 112) over the top of each tacking line, except for the outer frame. When complete, remove tacking threads from under feather stitch.

3 CROSS STITCH Tack centre lines onto each piece of scrap linen. Pin a piece of linen to the centre of every alternate division. Tack around all edges of linen through both layers, to secure. Graphs for cross stitch motifs are printed on page 94. Following graphs, work cross stitch motifs into the centre of each piece of linen, through both layers. Work each stitch using one strand of Appletons Crewel Wool over four threads of linen. Take care not to stitch into the threads of linen as they will be difficult to remove if they are split. End off embroidery thread securely on back of work. When the cross stitch is complete, work back stitch as indicated, using one strand of crewel wool.

4 REMOVING LINEN When all embroidery is complete, remove tacking threads from linen, and carefully pull the linen away, thread by thread, working slowly so as not to disturb the cross stitch. Use tweezers if necessary.

5 BACKING Pin cream cotton fabric to the wrong side of the embroidery to hide the back of the work. Slipstitch backing fabric into the 2.5cm margin around the edges (do not turn in raw edge as it will be covered by the hem).

6 HEM Turn in a double hem along each side of the blanket so that the tacked outer margin runs along the outer edge of the blanket. Stitch hem in place on the wrong side of the blanket, using cream machine thread. Thread the chenille needle with a long (approximately 80cm) length of Appletons 504 and work large blanket stitches around the outside edge. Remove any remaining tacking.

Graphs for Cross Stitched Cot Blanket

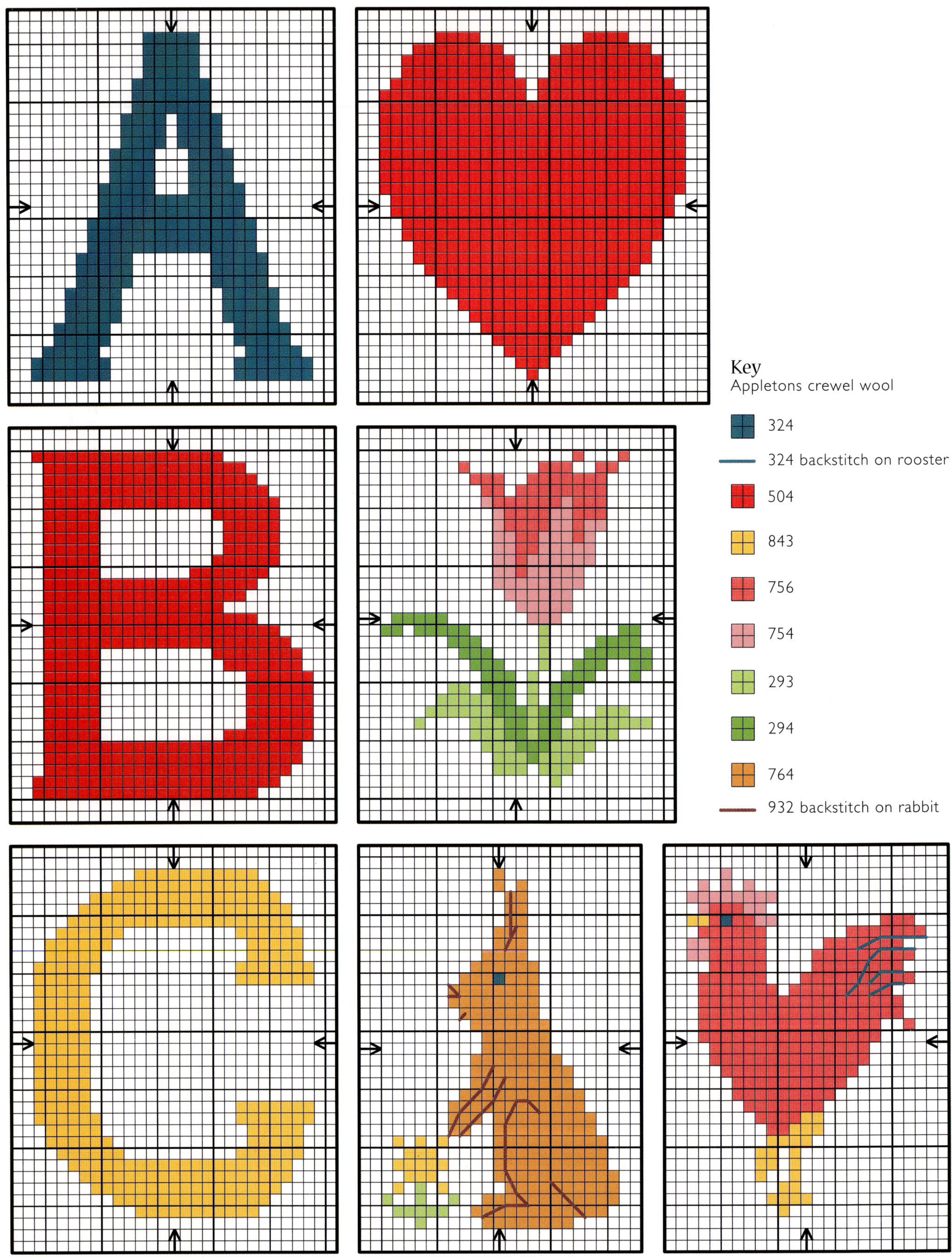

Instructions

Rag Doll

Page 47

Measurements

Finished doll measures approximately 30-35cm high.

Materials

- 35cm x 60cm natural-coloured rib knit
- Strong white thread, such as quilting or waxed thread
- Polyester fibrefill
- Knitting wool for hair
- Stranded embroidery cotton, for facial features
- Red pencil

Pattern pieces

Pattern pieces are printed on pattern sheet in pink. Trace Body 45, Arm 46 and Leg 48.

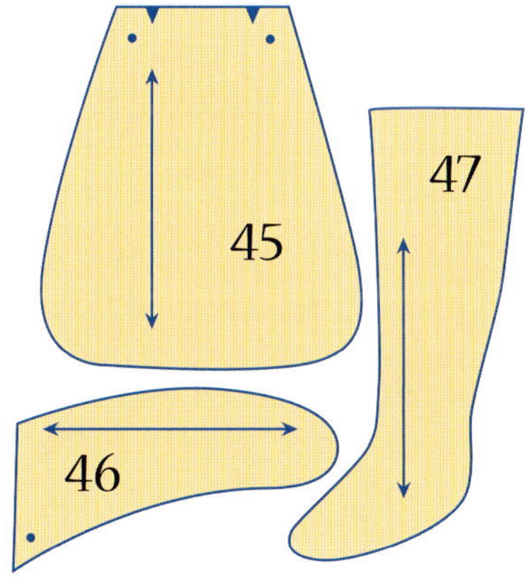

Cutting

NOTE 1cm seam allowance is **included** on all pieces and measurements unless otherwise indicated. When laying out the pieces, the rib should run vertically in the direction of the straight grain arrows. If your fabric is very lightweight or stretches too much, you will need to cut each piece twice, with the innermost layer cut with the maximum stretch running opposite to the outer layer. Note that rib knit does not have a right and wrong side.

From rib knit, cut two rectangles for the Head, each 13.5cm x 16cm, with the rib direction running parallel with the shorter edge. Cut also two Bodies, four Arms and four Legs.

Method

1 INNER HEAD The Head is made by stitching and filling one rectangle, then stretching the second rectangle over the top, for a smooth finish. Fold one Head rectangle in half crosswise, and stitch seam across short ends, allowing 1cm seam allowance. Using waxed thread (or double quilting thread) run a line of gathering stitches about 5mm from one open end, then pull up gathering as tightly as possible and tie off thread securely. This becomes the top of the Head. Turn Head right side out and stuff firmly with fibrefill. Using strong thread as before, run another line of gathering thread around lower edge, draw up tightly and secure. The Head should now roughly measure 10cm high, with a diameter of about 23.5cm. If your Head differs, try to correct it with more or less stuffing; otherwise it will be out of proportion to the Body.

Wind a length of strong thread around the Head, about 4.5cm from the top, draw up the ends firmly to create an indent for the eye sockets, then tie off ends securely. Use small stitches to anchor this thread in place at three or so points around the Head.

2 OUTER HEAD Stitch the remaining Head rectangle around the Head as smoothly as possible, folding and placing the seam at centre back, keeping the facial area as smooth as possible and ensuring that the raw edges and gathers at the top will be concealed by the hair. Wind thread around the lower edges to secure them together.

3 FACIAL FEATURES Using the diagram, below, as a guide, embroider the eyes along the eye socket line, placing them about 3cm apart, using three strands of thread and working in satin stitch (see **Embroidery Stitch Guide** on page 112). Working with a single strand of thread, embroider the mouth in the centre, 2.5cm below the eyes, using a couple of straight stitches. Use red pencil sparingly to create a little blush on the cheeks.

4 HAIR From knitting wool, cut a good hank of 50cm threads. Spread these out next to each other on your work surface. Take a long double length of wool and knot three or four strands of wool tightly together in the middle, then knot the next three, and so on for about 8cm, keeping all the knots as close as possible together. These knots form the central parting in the hair. Place the hair onto the Head and stitch in place along the centre parting, with a couple of stitches around the edge of the face as well. Plait the ends into two braids, tie with thread and trim the ends of the plaits evenly. Where necessary, use a couple of small stitches to keep hair firmly in place. To make the fringe, cut about six threads, each 8cm long. Bind these firmly in the middle with another piece of wool, then stitch the centre point to the parting, as photographed. Trim a little if necessary.

5 BODY Using a special stretch stitch or narrow zigzag, stitch Bodies together, leaving open between notches. Turn right side out, fill firmly with fibrefill, fold in raw edges around neck, then stitch Head firmly to Body, adding more stuffing as you work, to keep neck area firm.

6 ARMS & LEGS Stitch Arms and Legs together in pairs, leaving upper edges open. Turn right side out, fold in raw edges and slipstitch openings closed, folding upper edge of Legs so that centre back and front seams are in the middle. Stitch Arms and Legs firmly to Body.

Doll's Clothes

Materials

- 25cm x 45cm red checked cotton
- Small amount Velcro
- Embroidery thread
- Six buttons (optional)
- 25cm x 30cm red polar fleece or fleecy knit (see NOTE, below)
- 15cm x 20cm orange polar fleece or fleecy knit

NOTE You could also use washable felt to make the jacket and shoes.

Pattern pieces

Pattern pieces are printed on pattern sheet in pink. Trace Bodice Front 48, Bodice Back 49, Jacket Front 50, Pocket 51, Jacket Back 52, Sleeve 53, Collar 54 and Shoe 55. Heart outline for appliqué is printed in a pink tone.

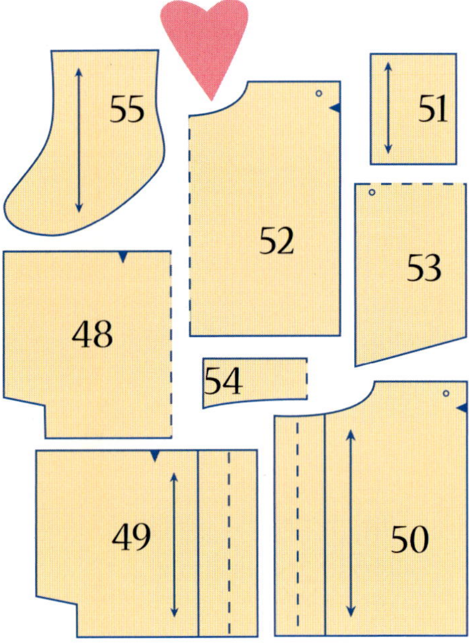

Cutting

NOTE 5mm seam allowance is included on Dress pieces and 1cm seam allowance is included on Jacket and Shoe pieces unless otherwise indicated.

From checked cotton, cut one Bodice Front and two Bodice Backs. Cut also one rectangle, 12cm x 40cm, for the Skirt.

From red fleece, cut two Jacket Fronts, one Pocket, one Jacket Back, two Sleeves and four Shoes.

From orange fleece, cut two Collars and one Heart.

Method

1 DRESS Finish raw edges on all pieces with a narrow zigzag. With right sides together, stitch Front to Backs at shoulder seams. Stitch a narrow hem on edges of sleeves. Fold under 1cm on opening edges of Backs and stitch in place. With right sides together, stitch sleeve and underarm seam in one operation. Press under and stitch raw edges of neck.

Stitch narrow hems on both short edges and one long edge of Skirt. Run a gathering thread along remaining raw edge, draw up Skirt to fit Bodice, stitch in place, then topstitch Bodice close to seamline.

Cut two 1cm pieces of Velcro and stitch to centre back opening. If using, trim back opening with two buttons. Fold under 5mm on raw edges of Heart and appliqué Heart to centre front of Bodice.

2 JACKET With right sides together, stitch Fronts to Back at shoulder seams. With right sides together, stitch Sleeves to Jacket, matching dots to shoulder seams. Stitch the Sleeve and side seam in one operation.

Turn in seam allowance and hem lower edge, Sleeves, centre front opening edges and upper edge of Pocket with running stitch in a contrast embroidery thread. Fold in remaining raw edges of Pocket and overcast in place with embroidery thread.

With right sides together, stitch Collars together leaving neck edge open. Turn right side out. Stitch one raw edge of Collar to neck edge of Jacket. Fold in raw edge on remaining edge of Collar and slipstitch in place over seam.

Cut two 1cm pieces of Velcro and stitch to centre front opening of Jacket. If using, trim front of Jacket with two buttons.

3 SHOES With right sides together, stitch Shoes together in pairs, leaving upper edge open. Turn right side out. Turn under 1cm on upper edge of each Shoe and secure hems in place using running stitch in contrast embroidery thread. If using, stitch a button to the outside of each Shoe, as photographed.

Soft Cloth Doll

Page 46

Measurements

Finished doll is approximately 25cm high.

Materials

- 25cm x 35cm stretch terry towelling for body
- 20cm x 20cm contrast stretch terry towelling for hat
- 15cm x 20cm skin-coloured rib knit
- 20cm ribbed tubing (see NOTE, below)
- 30-35g scoured sheep's wool (see NOTE, below)
- Strong thread, such as quilting thread
- Blue and red embroidery cotton
- Thin wool or cotton yarn for hair
- Embroidery needle
- Red chalk or coloured pencil

NOTE Scoured sheep's wool is wonderfully soft, but if it is not available, use polyester fibrefill and tease it out for extra softness. Ribbed tubing can sometimes be found in shops that specialise in knit fabrics, but if you can't find it, then cut a 20cm length from the leg of a pair of baby's tights. Alternatively, you can stitch a 5mm centre back seam in a 12cm x 20cm long piece of rib knit, turning it into a tube.

Pattern piece

Pattern piece is printed on pattern sheet in red. Trace Body 56.

56

Cutting

NOTE 1cm seam allowance is included on pattern piece and given measurements.

From stretchy towelling, cut two Bodies.

From contrast towelling, cut one rectangle, 16cm long 20cm wide, for Hat (greatest stretch running across width).

From skin-coloured rib, cut one rectangle, 13cm long x 17cm wide, for Head (greatest stretch running across width).

Method

NOTE Unless otherwise indicated, all seams are stitched with right sides together. Stitch all stretch fabrics with a stretch stitch or a narrow zigzag.

1 BODY Stitch Bodies together leaving neck edge open. Clip to within 3mm of stitching at angles in arms and legs. Turn Body right side out.

2 FEET & HANDS Tease out and fluff up the sheep's wool filling. Choose two even-sized pieces and stuff these into the end of the legs. Wind strong, thin thread around the outside of the legs, forming little ball-shaped feet, allowing any excess stuffing to protrude into the leg cavity. Secure the ends of the thread well and then "bury" them on the inside of the legs. Form the hands in the same way as the feet, but make them a little smaller.

3 DEFINING LIMBS Using double machine thread and following **Diagram 1**, make a line of tiny running stitch of about 9cm, from A to B, stitching through the front layer of fabric only. Take the needle from B back to A between the layers, pull up slightly, tie the ends off securely and "bury" the ends of the thread on the inside. Define the arms in the same way, stitching from C to D, for a length of about 3.5cm.

Diagram 1

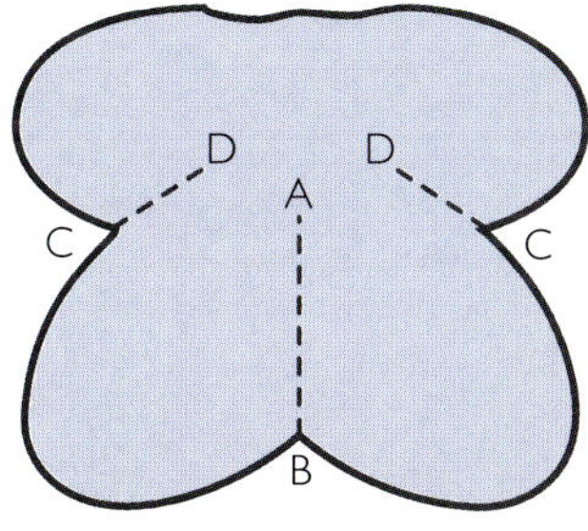

4 STUFFING You can add a little more stuffing to the Body at this point, or omit it completely, so that the finished doll is very soft and floppy.

5 INNER HEAD With strong thin thread, run a gathering thread around the upper edge of the ribbed tube, pull up the gathering very tightly, tie off, and turn tube right side out. Fill with wool stuffing until you have a firm ball shape with a circumference of about 14cm (see **Diagram 2**). Using strong thread, bind the Head below the stuffing firmly with strong thread, taking care to leave some fabric and stuffing protruding below the binding, to form the neck. Following **Diagram 3**, bind the lower edge of the Head to keep the neck stuffing in place, adding a little extra stuffing for firmness, if necessary.

Diagram 2

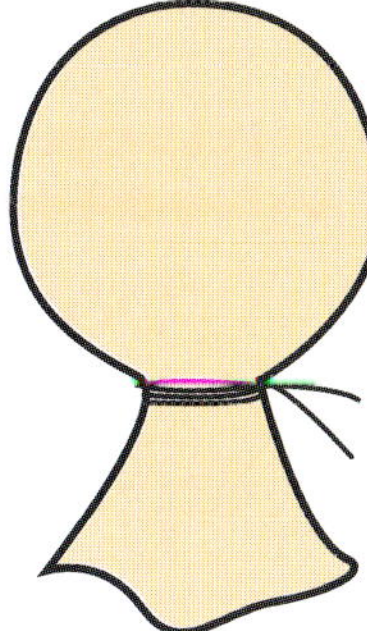

Diagram 3

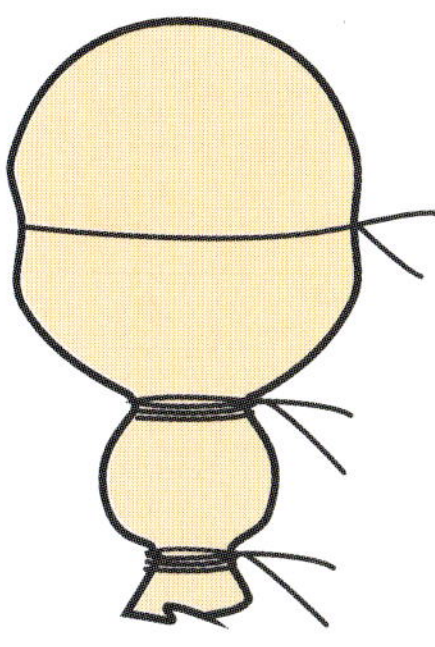

Using **Diagram 3** as a guide, wind a strong thread around the Head at the halfway point, to form the indentation for eye sockets. Pull this thread fairly tightly and knot the ends firmly. For the front of the Head, choose the side that looks most symmetrical, then slide the knot on the eye socket indentation around to the back and "bury" the threads.

6 OUTER HEAD Wrap the skin-coloured rectangle tautly around the Inner Head, with the rib running vertically. Cut away the excess fabric at the back, leaving about 2cm seam allowance. Remove the fabric from the Head, fold it in half, right sides together, and stitch to shape, following **Diagram 4**. Turn right side out and stretch it over the Inner Head with the seam at centre back. Take care that the rib is running evenly down the face and that there are no folds or pleats at the front. Wind strong thread below the Head to secure neck edge.

Diagram 4

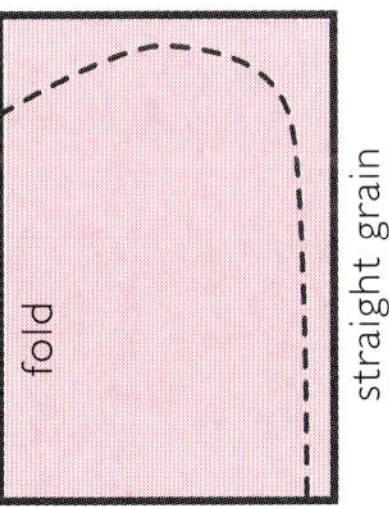

7 FACE Using pearl-headed pins, mark the positions of the eyes and mouth in a roughly equilateral triangle, placing the eyes along the indented socket line. Using strong double thread and starting from the back of the Head, push the needle through the Head to emerge at one of the eye pins. Take a small stitch and push the needle back through the Head to the starting point. Pull the thread slightly, to create an eye socket, tie off threads securely and "bury" ends. Repeat for second eye. Using blue embroidery thread, and anchoring it at the back of the head, work a small star in the eye socket, as photographed, by overlapping several straight stitches. Take the thread back to the back of the Head and tie off. Repeat for second eye. Stitch the mouth following **Diagram 5**: bring the thread from the back of the Head out at 1, then take it back into the Head at 2, but before pulling it taut, take a small stitch over the thread at 3, pulling the first stitch into a curve. Take thread to back of Head and tie off.

Diagram 5

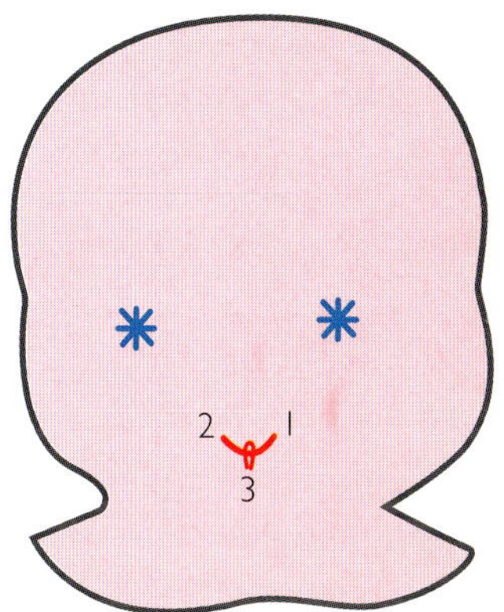

8 JOINING HEAD TO BODY Beginning at centre back and using strong thread, run a line of gathering stitches around the neck edge, folding in the seam allowance around neckline at the same time. Place the Head into the neck cavity of the Body, with the face to the front, pull up the gathering thread tightly

around the neck and secure the Head to the Body firmly with tiny stitches.

9 HAT Stretch the Hat rectangle around the Head with the rib running vertically (greatest stretch around Head). Cut away excess fabric at the back, leaving 2cm seam allowance. With right sides together, stitch centre back seam of Hat (see **Diagram 6**), leaving ends open. Wind strong thread around one open end, about 1cm from the edge, and tie off securely. Turn Hat right side out. Turn in 1cm on lower edge, stretch this edge over Head with seam at centre back and slipstitch in place with tiny stitches.

Diagram 6

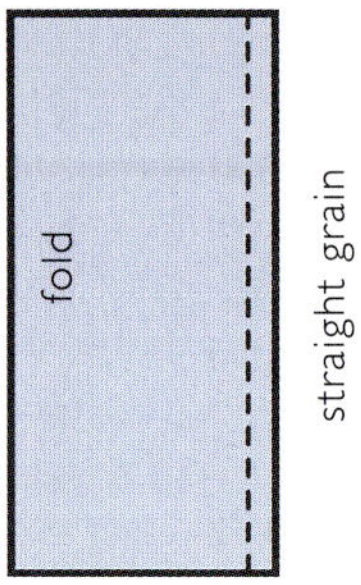

fold

straight grain

10 HAIR Thread a needle with a double length of wool or cotton yarn. Starting on the righthand side of **Diagram 7** and working close to the edge of the Hat, push the needle into the fabric at 1, and take it behind the fabric to re-emerge at 2 (about 1cm away), leaving approximately 1cm of thread extending at 1. Now reinsert the needle at 1 (3), and bring it out again at 4, halfway between 1 and 2. Pull the thread tight and cut off, about 1cm from the fabric. Begin the next stitch at point 2 of the previous stitch and work around the edge of the Hat in this way, creating a fringe of hair.

Diagram 7

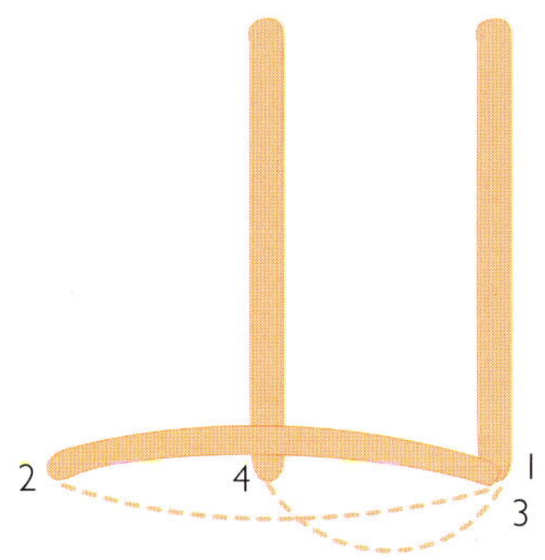

11 FINISHING Colour the cheeks with a little red chalk or coloured pencil.

12 WASHING Finished dolls may be handwashed in warm water using a wool detergent. Don't soak for too long. Spin the doll in a spin dryer to remove excess water but do not tumble dry. Pull the doll back into shape and allow to dry. Take care that the temperature of the water does not vary too much or the wool may felt.

Trousers

Page 19

Measurements

*To fit baby aged 6 (**12**, 18) months. Finished length is approximately 37 (**42**, 49)cm.*

Materials

- 1.1m x 115cm yellow/white stripe
- 10cm x 30cm each of plain orange and white fabric
- 10cm x 30cm iron-on interfacing
- 10cm x 30cm double-sided appliqué webbing, such as Vliesofix
- Yellow, orange and white machine thread
- Contrast embroidery cotton, optional
- 0.6m x 20mm-wide elastic
- Two x 12mm-diameter white buttons
- 10mm-diameter ring snap fasteners

Pattern pieces

Pattern pieces are printed on pattern sheet in black. Appliqué outlines are also on the pattern sheet. Trace Front/Back 1, Pocket 2, Front Waistband 3, Back Waistband 4 and Crotch Band 5. From the appliqué outlines, trace Moon and Star motifs.

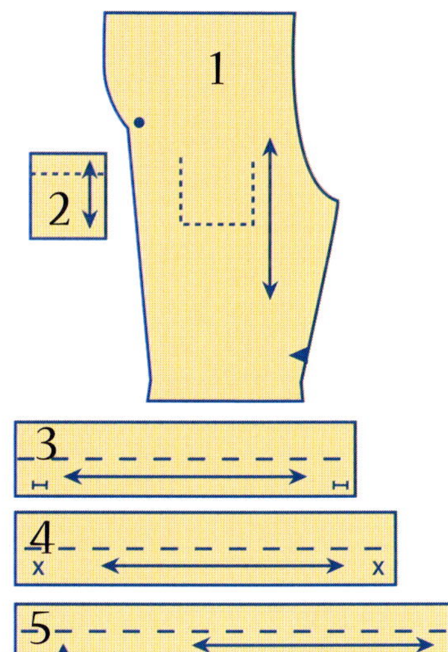

Cutting

NOTE 1.5cm seam allowance is **included** on all pieces unless otherwise indicated. 3cm hem allowance is included on lower edge. Appliqué outlines do not need seam allowance.

From yellow/white stripe fabric, cut four Pants Front/Backs, two Pockets, one Front Waistband, one Back Waistband and two Crotch Bands.

From orange fabric, cut two x 10cm squares.

From white fabric, cut two x 10cm squares.

From interfacing, cut one Crotch Band. Fold in half lengthwise and cut along fold line, forming two pieces of Crotch Band interfacing.

Refer to **Basic Appliqué Techniques** on page 118, then trace appliqué outlines onto double-sided appliqué webbing. Apply Star to a scrap of white fabric and Moon to a scrap of orange fabric, then cut out accurately.

Method

Unless otherwise indicated, all seams are stitched with right sides together.

1 APPLIQUÉ Remove backing paper and press Moon motif onto centre of one white square, and Star motif onto centre of one orange square. With colour-coordinated thread, stitch each motif in position using a close, narrow zigzag.

With right sides together, stitch each square to its matching backing square, allowing 5mm seams and leaving an opening for turning. Turn right side out, slipstitch opening closed and press. Position a square on each Trousers Front and zigzag in place. Outline with decorative embroidery stitch in contrast colour, if desired.

2 POCKETS Press under 5mm on uppper edge of each Pocket. With right sides together, fold upper edge of Pocket to outside along fold line and stitch at sides, forming facing. Fold facing back to inside and press. Topstitch 2mm from finished edge and again, 1cm from first stitching. Press under seam allowance on remaining raw edges of Pockets. Topstitch Pockets to Trouser Backs, as indicated, reinforcing with diagonal stitching at upper corners.

3 CENTRE FRONT/BACK SEAMS Stitch centre front seam of Trouser Fronts. Stitch centre back seam of Trouser Backs. Stitch curved areas again, close to original stitching, to reinforce seam. Trim and clip curves. Press seams open.

4 SIDE SEAMS Stitch Front to Back at sides, leaving open above dot on each side.Press under 1cm on self facings on Front and stitch. Press under 1cm on raw edge of self facings on Back, then turn under another 1cm and stitch. Press self facings towards front and, with narrow zigzag, stitch horizontally across seam allowance at top of seam to reinforce opening. If desired, topstitch seams 2mm from seam line.

5 WAISTBANDS Stitch Front Waistband to Trousers Front, ensuring that the self facings lie folded flat and that the ends of the Band extend 1.5cm at each side. Press under the seam allowance on long raw edge and ends of Waistband. Fold Waistband in half lengthwise, wrong sides together, and slipstitch folded edge over seam, leaving ends open. Repeat process for Back Waistband. On outside, topstitch close to seam and upper edge of both Waistbands.

6 ELASTIC Cut two pieces of elastic, each 20cm long (or to fit). Thread first piece of elastic through Front Waistband and anchor approximately 4cm from end by stitching across Waistband several times. Anchor remaining end of elastic in the same way, making sure to do this 4cm in from edge. Repeat this process for Back Waistband. Topstitch ends of each Waistband 2mm from edge. Work a buttonhole at each end of Front Waistband and sew on buttons to Back Waistband to correspond.

7 HEMS Press under 5mm on lower edge of each Trouser leg, then press under another 2.5cm and machine-stitch the hems in place.

8 CROTCH BANDS Cut away seam allowance from Crotch Band interfacing and fuse to one half of each Crotch Band. Stitch one Crotch Band to crotch edge of Trousers Front, with 1.5cm seam allowance extending at each end. Press under seam allowance along long edge of Band. Fold Band in half lengthwise, right sides together, and stitch across ends. Turn Band to right side and stitch close to pressed edge. Repeat for back Crotch Band. Attach evenly-spaced ring snap fasteners to Crotch Bands, following the manufacturer's instructions.

Sailor Cap

Page 18

Measurements

To fit baby aged 6 (12, 18) months.
*Head circumference: 44 (***47***, 49) cm.*

Materials

- 0.2m x 115cm red stripe
- 0.4m x 115cm white fabric
- 0.4m iron-on interfacing
- Scraps of both orange and red fabric, for appliqué
- Small scrap double-sided appliqué webbing, such as Vliesofix
- Orange, red and white machine thread
- Red stranded embroidery cotton

Pattern pieces

Pattern pieces are printed on pattern sheet in black. Appliqué outlines are also on the pattern sheet. Trace Crown 6 and Brim 7. Trace Fish appliqué motif.

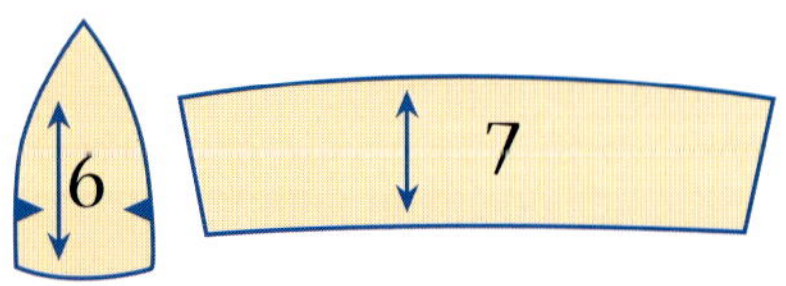

Cutting

NOTE 1.5cm seam allowance is **included** on pattern pieces unless otherwise indicated. Appliqué outline does not need seam allowance.

From red stripe, cut six Crowns.

From white fabric, cut six Crowns and two Brims.

From interfacing, cut six Crowns and one Brim.

Refer to **Basic Appliqué Techniques** on page 118, then trace appliqué outline onto double-sided appliqué webbing. Apply Fish to a scrap of orange fabric and Fish Fin to a scrap of plain red fabric, then cut out accurately.

Method

Unless otherwise indicated, all seams are stitched with right sides together.

1 APPLIQUÉ Remove backing paper and apply Fish and Fin to centre of one Brim, taking care that you get it the right way up. (Remember Brim will be turned up around finished hat.) Zigzag in place with orange and red thread, as appropriate, then add details with red embroidery thread, using stem stitch and satin stitch (see **Embroidery Stitch Guide** on page 112). Set aside.

2 CROWN Remove points from interfacing Crowns, to avoid bulk, then apply interfacing to wrong side of six striped Crown sections. (White Crown sections, which are not interfaced, become crown lining.) Matching notches, stitch striped Crown sections together in threes, forming two half crowns. Trim seams to 7mm and press seams open. Pin the two half crown sections together, matching points, then stitch, forming complete crown. Trim seam and press open.

Repeat for crown lining. Place crown lining into crown, wrong sides together and matching seams and raw edges, and baste raw edges together.

3 BRIM Apply interfacing to wrong side of appliquéd Brim. (Remaining Brim becomes Brim lining.) Stitch short ends of Brim together, forming a circle. Press seam open. Repeat for Brim lining.

With seams matching, stitch Brim to Brim lining around outside (longer) edge. Trim seam, clip curves, turn completed Brim right side out and press.

4 JOIN BRIM TO CROWN With right side of Brim lining facing right side of striped Crown, stitch Brim lining to Crown, taking care to keep remaining raw edge of Brim out of seam. (This might seem wrong, but remember that completed Brim is to be turned up around hat like a cuff.) Press under seam allowance on raw edge of Brim and topstitch in place over seam, stitching close to pressed edge. Topstitch close to outer edge of Brim, then turn Brim up to outside.

Nursery Hold-All

Page 59

Measurements

Finished hold-all measures 14cm x 45cm.

Materials

- 10cm x 97cm cream or white Aida cloth, 18-count
- One skein each red and black stranded embroidery cotton
- 0.2m x 90cm red fabric with black spots, or a red print
- 14cm x 45cm firm, iron-on interfacing
- 10cm x 97cm cream or white lining fabric
- 2.4m ready-made bias binding (we used red)

Method

1 PLEAT LINES To mark pleat lines on Aida cloth, working from one end of the strip, place a pin 5cm from the edge, then another *2.5cm from the first pin, the next 8cm from the last, the next 2.5cm away, and the next 5.5cm. Repeat from * three times, then place the last three pins in reverse order to the first three, that is, 2.5cm, 8cm, 2.5cm, and the distance from the last pin to the edge should be 5cm. Mark the positions of these pins with a vertical basting thread. The five 8cm sections will form the pocket fronts.

2 EMBROIDERY Using two strands of thread, working across two squares at a time and following the graph, on page 59, cross stitch a ladybird to the centre of each 8cm section (five in all). Press lightly on the back when finished.

3 BACKING From red spotted fabric, cut two rectangles, each 14cm x 45cm. Apply interfacing to wrong side of one rectangle. With wrong sides together, pin second red rectangle to the first around all edges, trim the corners to round them slightly, then baste raw edges together.

4 LINING With wrong sides together, baste plain lining rectangle to Aida cloth around raw edges. Cut a piece of bias binding 97cm long. Open out one long edge of binding and, with right sides together, stitch edge of binding to top edge of Aida. Turn remaining edge of binding to inside and slipstitch in place over seam.

5 PLEATS Press pleats in Aida cloth, following pleat markings, so that you end up with five 8cm box pleats that will form pockets. Baste across top and bottom edges of cloth to hold pleats in positon. Baste Aida cloth to lower edge of red spotted backing, rounding the Aida corners at the lower edge, to match backing. Make a vertical line of stitching down the middle of each of the 5.5cm sections of Aida cloth to secure pockets to backing, taking care not to catch the edges of the pleats. Pull threads to the back of the work and tie off firmly.

6 BINDING Make two loops of bias binding, each 4cm long when folded, and attach to upper corners of backing. With right sides together, open out and stitch one edge of bias binding around the outside edge of the hold-all, securing loops and raw edges of Aida cloth at the same time. Fold under raw edges of binding neatly at join. Turn remaining edge of binding to the back and slipstitch in place over seam. Remove basting from pleats.

Ladybird Appliqué

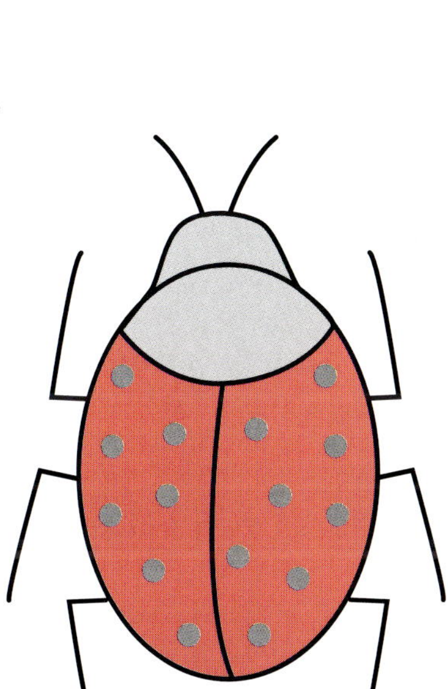

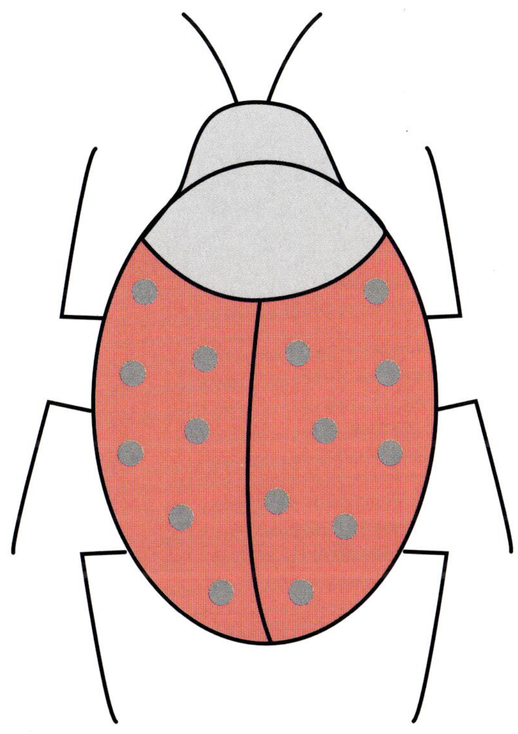

Back view

Romper

Page 23

Measurements

*To fit baby aged 6 (**12**, 18) months. Finished length of Romper is approximately 42 (**45**, 48)cm.*

Materials

- 0.6m x 115cm blue/white check
- 0.4m x 90cm contrast print, for lining
- 0.3m x 90cm iron-on interfacing
- 0.6m x 12mm-wide elastic
- 0.3m popper tape (for crotch opening)
- Six small buttons

Pattern pieces

Pattern pieces are printed on pattern sheet in black. Trace Bodice Front 8, Bodice Back 9, Waist Tab 11, Pants Front/Back 12, Leg Band 13 and Crotch Band 14.

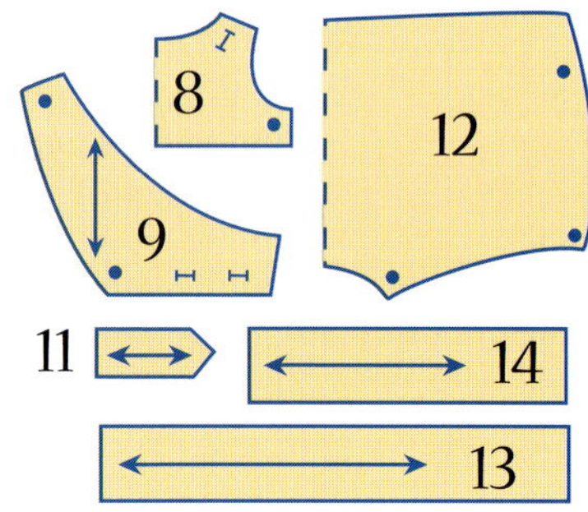

Cutting

NOTE 1.5cm seam allowance is **included** on all pieces unless otherwise indicated.

From blue/white check, cut one Bodice Front, two Bodice Backs, two Waist Tabs, two Pants Front/Backs, two Leg Bands and two Crotch Bands.

From contrast print, cut one Bodice Front, two Bodice Backs and two Waist Tabs.

From interfacing, cut one Bodice Front, two Bodice Backs and two Waist Tabs.

Method

Unless otherwise indicated, all seams are stitched with right sides together.

1 INTERFACING Apply interfacing to wrong side of main fabric Waist Tabs, Bodice Front and Bodice Backs.

2 WAIST TABS Stitch interfaced Waist Tab to Waist Tab lining in pairs, allowing 5mm seams, and leaving short straight end open. Trim corners, turn right side out and press. Topstitch Tabs close to all finished edges. With raw edges even, baste Waist Tabs to each side of Bodice Front, between given symbols.

3 BODICE FRONT & LINING Stitch interfaced Bodice Front to Bodice Front lining, sandwiching Tabs as basted and leaving lower edge open. Trim seam and corners, clip curves, turn right side out and press.

4 BODICE BACK & LINING Stitch interfaced Bodice Back to Bodice Back lining in pairs, leaving open along waist edge from side to centre back dot. Trim seam and corners, clip curves. Turn Bodice Back right side out and press.

5 PANTS Pin and stitch Romper Pants side seams, leaving open above small dot on each side. Press seams open and neaten. Handstitch a narrow hem on opening edges of each side. Run a gathering thread along front and back waist edge of Pants.

6 JOINING PANTS TO BODICE FRONT Pin waist edge of Pants front to Bodice Front, matching centres. Pull up gathers to fit and stitch, taking care not to catch Bodice Front lining in seam. Trim seam and press towards Bodice. Fold under raw edge on Bodice Front lining and slipstitch folded edge in place over seam.

7 JOINING PANTS TO BODICE BACK Pin waist edge of Pants back to each Bodice Back, carefully matching centre backs. Note that Bodices overlap each other at centre back. Pull up gathers to fit and stitch, taking care not to catch lining or remaining section of Bodice in seam. Trim seam and press towards Bodice. Fold under raw edge on Bodice Back linings and slipstitch folded edges in place over seam.

8 FINISHING BODICE Topstitch close to all finished edges of Bodice Front and Back. Following markings on pattern pieces, work two buttonholes in Bodice Front, and two buttonholes along waist edge at each end of Bodice Back. Sew buttons to Bodice Back and Waist Tabs, to correspond.

9 LEG BANDS Run a gathering thread along lower edge of each leg, between small dots. With raw edges even, pin leg edge to Leg Band and draw up gathers to fit. Do not allow for overlap at each end, as Crotch Bands will cover raw edges. Stitch. Trim seam to 5mm. Press under seam allowance on remaining raw edge of Leg Bands and trim allowance to 5mm. Fold Band to inside and slipstitch pressed edge over seam. On outside, topstitch close to seam. Cut elastic to fit and thread through Leg Band casings, catching ends of elastic firmly in place at each end of casing.

10 CROTCH BANDS Stitch each crotch edge of Pants to a Crotch Band, allowing 1.5cm to extend at each end on each Band. Trim seam to 5mm. Press under seam allowance on remaining long raw edge of Crotch Bands and trim seam allowance to 5mm. Fold Band in half, right sides together, and stitch across short ends. Trim seams. Turn Band back to inside and slipstitch folded edge in place over seam. Cut popper tape to fit Crotch Band and stitch one half to inside edge of front Crotch Band, turning under raw ends. Stitch remaining half of tape to outside edge of back Crotch Band.

Sundress

Page 22

Measurements

*To fit baby aged 6 (**12**, 18) months. Finished length of Sundress is approximately 45 (**50**, 55)cm.*

Materials

- 1m x 90cm floral print
- 0.3m x 90cm iron-on interfacing
- Six small buttons

Pattern pieces

Pattern pieces are printed on pattern sheet in black. Trace Bodice Front 8, Bodice Back 9, Skirt Front/Back 10 and Waist Tab 11.

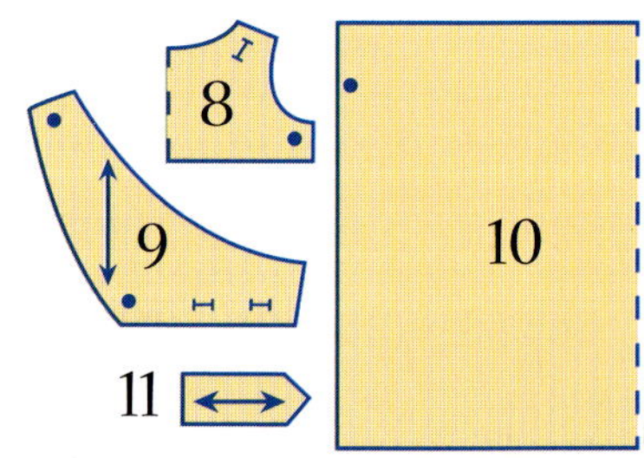

Cutting

NOTE 1.5cm seam allowance is **included** on all pieces unless otherwise indicated. 5cm hem allowance is also included on the lower edge of Skirt.

From floral print, cut two Bodice Fronts, four Bodice Backs, four Waist Tabs and two Skirts.

From interfacing, cut one Bodice Front, two Bodice Backs and two Waist Tabs.

Method

Unless otherwise indicated, all seams are stitched with right sides together.

1 INTERFACING Apply interfacing to wrong side of two Waist Tabs, one Bodice Front and two Bodice Backs. Remaining sections become lining.

2 BODICE Construct Bodice Front and Backs as for Romper, **Steps 2** to **4**, opposite.

3 SKIRT Pin and stitch Skirt side seams, leaving open above small dots on each side. Press seams open and neaten. Handstitch a narrow hem on opening edges of each side. Run a gathering thread along front and back waist edges of Skirt.

4 ATTACHING SKIRT TO BODICE Attach the waist edges of the Skirt to Bodice Front and Backs as for Romper, **Steps 6** & **7**, opposite.

5 FINISHING BODICE Finish as for Romper, **Step 8**, opposite.

6 HEM Finish lower edge of Skirt with a handstitched hem.

Bloomers

Page 22

Measurements

To fit baby aged 6 to 18 months (one size).

Materials

- 0.3m x 90cm floral print
- 1.2m x 7mm-wide elastic

Pattern piece

Pattern piece is printed on pattern sheet in black. Trace Bloomers Front/Back 15.

Cutting

NOTE 1.5cm seam allowance and 2.5cm casing allowance are **included** on pattern piece.

From floral print, cut two Front/Backs.

Method

Unless otherwise indicated, all seams are stitched with right sides together.

1 INSIDE LEG & CROTCH SEAMS Pin, stitch and neaten inside leg seams. Place one leg inside the other, right sides together, and stitch crotch seam from centre front to centre back, matching inside leg seams.

2 CASING Press under 1cm on casing edges, then press under another 1.5cm and stitch close to both edges, leaving an opening for elastic. Cut elastic to fit, thread through casings, secure ends and stitch openings closed.

Sunhat

Page 22

Measurements

*To fit baby aged 6 (**12**, 18) months.*
*Head circumference 44 (**47**, 49)cm.*

Materials

- 0.5m x 90cm blue/white check
- 0.5m x 90cm floral print
- 0.5m x 90cm iron-on interfacing

Pattern pieces

Pattern pieces are printed on the pattern sheet in black. Trace Crown 16, Side 17 and Brim 18.

Cutting

NOTE 1.5cm seam allowance is **included** on all the pattern pieces and given measurements, unless otherwise indicated.

From blue/white check, cut one Crown, one Side and one Brim.

From floral print, cut one Crown, one Side and one Brim. Cut also two strips, each 3.5cm x 45cm, for Ties.

From interfacing, cut one Crown, one Side and two Brims.

Method

Unless otherwise indicated, all seams are stitched with right sides together.

1 INTERFACING Apply interfacing to wrong side of all blue/white check pieces and to wrong side of floral Brim. Floral print pieces become lining.

2 SIDE Stay-stitch Side section along long unnotched edge and make a series of clips across seam allowance to stitching. Stitch centre back seam of Side. Press seam open and topstitch close to seam on each side. Construct Side lining in the same way.

3 CROWN With raw edges even and matching small dots to centre front and back, pin Crown to Side. Stitch seam and trim. Topstitch upper edge of Side, close to seam. Join Crown lining to Side lining in the same way.

4 BRIM Stitch centre back seam of both Brim and Brim lining. Press seams open and topstitch close to seam on each side. Stitch Brim to Brim lining around outer edge, matching centre front and back. Trim seam, clip curves, turn right side out and press. Topstitch 1cm from finished edge. Baste raw edges of Brim together.

5 JOINING BRIM TO SIDE Pin Brim to Side, matching centre front and back. Stitch, taking care not to catch Side lining in seam. Trim seam, clip curves and press seam allowance towards Side.

6 TIES Press under 1cm on raw edges of each Tie, then fold Ties in half lengthwise, wrong sides together, and stitch close to all edges. Position Ties on inside of hat, on seam allowance of Side and Brim, as indicated, and baste in place. On outside, topstitch lower edge of Side close to seam, sandwiching Ties at the same time. Tie a knot in remaining ends of Ties, if you wish.

7 FINISHING Turn under seam allowance on Side lining and slipstitch folded edge in place over seam.

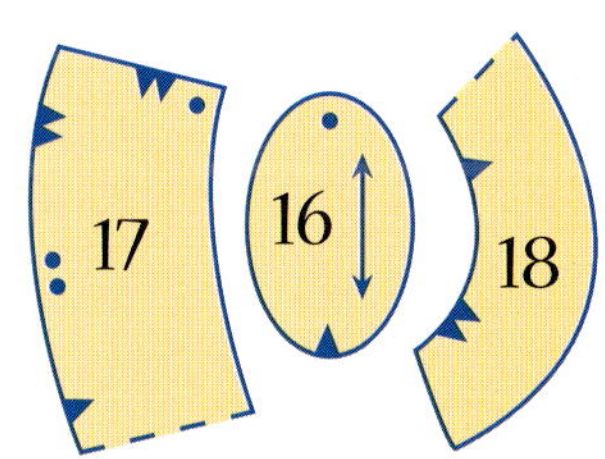

Embroidered Tunic

Page 22

Measurements

*To fit baby aged 3 (**6**, 12) months. Fits chest: 40 (**45**, 52.5)cm. Actual measurement: 44 (**50**, 58.5)cm; length: 24 (**28**, 33)cm; sleeve length: 13 (**16**, 21)cm.*

Materials

Panda Regal 4-ply (50g):

- 3 (**3**, 4) balls
- One pair each 2.75mm (No 12) and 3.25mm (No 10) knitting needles
- Two stitch-holders
- DMC Stranded Embroidery Cotton: one skein each of four colours for embroidery on white Tunic, or two skeins of white for embroidery on blue Tunic
- Knitter's needle for sewing seams and embroidery

Tension

See **Knitting and Crochet Notes** on page 120.
27 sts and 34 rows to 10cm over st st, using 3.25mm needles.

BACK

Using 3.25mm needles, cast on 61 (**69**, 81) sts.
Work 16 rows st st.
****Beg patt. 1st row.** K2 (**3**, 3), *yfwd, K3, pass yfwd over K3 just worked; rep from * to last 2 (**3**, 3) sts, K2 (**3**, 3).
2nd row. Purl.
3rd row. K3 (**1**, 1), *yfwd, K3, pass yfwd over K3 just worked; rep from * to last 1 (**2**, 2) st/s, K1 (**2**, 2).
4th row. Purl.
5th row. As 1st row.**
Work 17 rows st st, beg with a purl row.
Last 22 rows form patt.
Cont in patt until work measures 22 (**26**, 31)cm from beg, ending with a wrong-side row.
Shape Back neck. Next row. Patt 20 (**23**, 28) sts, *turn.*
Keeping patt correct on these 20 (**23**, 28) sts, dec one st at neck edge in every row until 15 (**18**, 23) sts rem.
Shape shoulder. Cast off 7 (**9**, 11) sts at beg of next row.
Work one row.
Cast off rem 8 (**9**, 12) sts.
With right side facing, sl next 21 (**23**, 25) sts on a stitch-holder and leave. Join yarn to rem 20 (**23**, 28) sts and patt to end.
Work as from *** to ***.
Work one row.
Shape shoulder. Complete as given for other shoulder.

FRONT

Work as for Back until there are 14 rows less than Back to beg of shoulder shaping, thus ending with a wrong-side row.
Shape neck. Next row. Patt 21 (**24**, 29) sts, *turn.*
****Keeping patt correct on these 21 (**24**, 29) sts, dec one st at neck edge in alt rows until 15 (**18**, 23) sts rem.
Work one row.****
Shape shoulder. Work as for Back shoulder shaping.
With right side facing, sl next 19 (**21**, 23) sts on a stitch-holder and leave. Join yarn to rem 21 (**24**, 29) sts and patt to end.
Work as from **** to ****.
Work one row.
Shape shoulder. Complete as for other shoulder.

SLEEVES

Using 3.25mm needles, cast on 43 (**45**, 45) sts.
Work 16 rows st st, inc one st at each end of 3rd (**5th**, 5th) and foll alt rows until there are 57 sts.
Beg patt. Working in patt as given for **Size 6 months** of Back, and working extra sts into patt, inc one st at each end of next and foll alt row, then in foll 4th rows until there are 67 (**73**, 81) sts.
Cont straight in patt until work measures 13 (**16**, 21)cm from beg, ending with a wrong-side row.
Shape top. Keeping patt correct, cast off 8 (**9**, 10) sts at beg of next 4 rows, then 9 (**9**, 10) sts at beg of foll 2 rows.
Cast off rem 17 (**19**, 21) sts.

BACK NECK EDGING

With right side facing and using 2.75mm needles, knit up 31 (**33**, 35) sts evenly along Back neck, incl sts from stitch-holder.
Knit one row.
Cast off purlways.

FRONT NECK EDGING

With right side facing and using 2.75mm needles, knit up 41 (**43**, 45) sts evenly along Front neck, incl sts from stitch-holder.
Knit one row.
Cast off purlways.

FRONT LOWER EDGING

With right side facing and using 2.75mm needles, knit up 61 (**69**, 81) sts evenly along lower edge of Front.
Knit one row.
Cast off purlways.

BACK LOWER EDGING

Work as for Front Lower Edging.

SLEEVE EDGING

With right side facing and using 2.75mm needles, knit up 43 (**45**, 45) sts evenly along lower edge of Sleeve.
Knit one row.
Cast off purlways.

To make up

Join shoulder and Edging seams. Tie a marker 12 (**13**, 15)cm down from beg of shoulder shaping on side edges of Back and Front to mark armholes. Sew in Sleeves evenly between markers, placing centre of Sleeves to shoulder seams. Join side, Sleeve and Edging seams. Using six strands DMC Stranded Cotton and stem stitch and lazy daisy stitch (see **Embroidery Stitch Guide** on page 112), embroider flowers to stocking stitch sections, as photographed.

Vest, Hat and Moccasins

Page 23

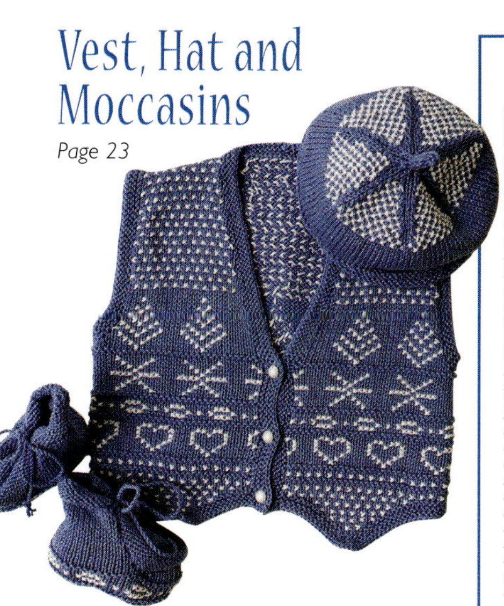

Measurements

*To fit baby aged 3 (**6**, 12) months.*
*Fits chest: 40 (**45**, 52.5)cm.* ***Vest*** *actual measurement: 44 (**50**, 59)cm; length: 20 (**24**, 29)cm.* ***Hat*** *fits head approximately 40 (**45**, 50)cm.* ***Moccasins*** *fit foot 8-9cm.*

Materials

Panda Regal 4-ply (50g):

- 2 (**2**, 3) balls for **Vest**
- 1 ball (all sizes) for **Hat**
- 1 ball for **Moccasins**
- One pair each 2.75mm (No 12) and 3.25mm (No 10) knitting needles
- One set of 3.25mm (No 10) knitting needles for **Hat**
- Knitter's needle for sewing seams and embroidery
- DMC Stranded Cotton: one skein each of lilac and green, two skeins of red and four skeins of gold for embroidery on white Vest, and nine skeins of white for blue vest
- Three buttons for **Vest**
- Two stitch-holders for **Moccasins**

Tension

See **Knitting and Crochet Notes** on page 120.
27 sts and 34 rows to 10cm over st st, using 3.25mm needles.

Graph for Vest

Rows 12–68 (rep these 4 rows for rem. — rows 65–68)

Beg Back (row 13)

Left Front Edge

Centre st for Back

3 6 12 Side Edge of Back and Left Front

Key

☐ = Knit st on odd numbered rows (right side), purl st on even numbered rows (wrong side).

⊡ = Knit st on even numbered rows (wrong side).

☒ = DMC stranded cotton and 'Cross stitch' embroidered on afterwards in colour/s as pictured.

NOTE When working from Graph for Back, work each row from side edge to centre st, then back to side edge, working centre st only once. When working from Graph for Left Front, read odd numbered rows (right side) from right to left and even numbered rows (wrong side) from left to right.

VEST

BACK

Using 2.75mm needles, cast on 61 (**69**, 81) sts.

Knit 5 rows garter st (1st row is wrong side). Change to 3.25mm needles.

Beg patt from Graph. Work rows 13 to 38 (**48**, 58) incl from Graph as indicated for Back.

Shape armholes. Keeping patt from Graph correct, cast off 3 (**3**, 4) sts at beg of next 2 rows...55 (**63**, 73) sts.

Dec one st at each end of next and foll alt row/s until 51 (**57**, 65) sts rem.

Work a further 35 (**37**, 41) rows from Graph.

Shape shoulders. Keeping Graph patt correct, cast off 5 (**6**, 7) sts at beg of next 6 rows.

Cast off rem 21 (**21**, 23) sts.

LEFT FRONT

Using 3.25mm needles, cast on 2 sts.

Work rows 1 to 14 incl from Graph as indicated for Left Front...30 (**34**, 40) sts.

Work a further 24 (**34**, 44) rows from Graph.

Shape armhole and front slope. Next row. Keeping Graph patt correct, cast off 3 (**3**, 4) sts, patt to last 2 sts, K2tog...26 (**30**, 35) sts.

Keeping patt from Graph correct, dec one st at armhole edge in foll alt rows 2 (**3**, 4) times, *AT THE SAME TIME* dec one st at end (front edge) in foll 4th rows 9 (**9**, 10) times...15 (**18**, 21) sts.

Work 3 (**7**, 9) rows from Graph.

Shape shoulder. Cast off 5 (**6**, 7) sts at beg of next row and foll alt row.

Work one row.

Cast off rem 5 (**6**, 7) sts.

RIGHT FRONT

Work to correspond with Left Front, reversing all shapings and Graph.

RIGHT FRONT LOWER BAND

With right side facing, using 2.75mm needles and beg at side edge, knit up 14 (**18**, 24) sts evenly along side edge of peak, one st in centre of peak (centre st), then 14 sts evenly along rem side of peak...29 (**33**, 39) sts.
Knit 5 rows garter st, inc one st at either side of centre st in every row...39 (**43**, 49) sts.
Cast off loosely.

LEFT FRONT LOWER BAND

With right side facing, using 2.75mm needles and beg at front edge, knit up 14 sts evenly along side edge of peak, one st in centre of peak (centre st), then 14 (**18**, 24) sts evenly along rem side of peak to side edge...29 (**33**, 39) sts. Complete to correspond with Right Front Lower Band.

RIGHT FRONT BAND

Join shoulder seams. With right side facing and using 2.75mm needles, knit up 22 (**30**, 40) sts evenly along Right Front edge to beg of front slope shaping, 40 (**44**, 50) sts evenly along shaped edge to shoulder, then 10 (**10**, 11) sts evenly across half of Back neck...72 (**84**, 101) sts.
Knit one row.
2nd row. K3, *yfwd (to make a st), K2tog, K6 (**10**, 15), rep from * once more, yfwd (to make a st), K2tog, knit to end...3 buttonholes.
Knit 3 rows garter st.
Cast off loosely.

LEFT FRONT BAND

With right side facing and using 2.75mm needles, knit up 10 (**10**, 11) sts evenly across half of Back neck, 40 (**44**, 50) sts along shaped edge, then 22 (**30**, 40) sts evenly along rem of front edge...72 (**84**, 101) sts.
Knit 5 rows garter st.
Cast off loosely.

ARMBANDS

With right side facing and using 2.75mm needles, knit up 65 (**71**, 79) sts evenly along armhole edge.
Knit 5 rows garter st.
Cast off loosely.

To make up

Join side and Armband seams. Join centre Back neck seam. Using six strands DMC Stranded Cotton and cross stitch, embroider motifs from Graph to Back and Fronts in colour/s as pictured. Sew on buttons.

HAT

Using set of 3.25mm needles, cast 90 (**102**, 114) sts evenly onto 3 needles.
Purl 5 rnds.
Knit 27 (**29**, 31) rnds.
Shape crown. 1st rnd. K5 (**6**, 7), *sl 1, K1, psso, K1, K2tog, K10 (**12**, 14); rep from * to last 10 (**11**, 12) sts, sl 1, K1, psso, K1, K2tog, K5 (**6**, 7)...78 (**90**, 102) sts.
2nd and alt rnds. Knit.
3rd rnd. K4 (**5**, 6), *sl 1, K1, psso, K1, K2tog, K8 (**10**, 12); rep from * to last 9 (**10**, 11) sts, sl 1, K1, psso, K1, K2tog, K4 (**5**, 6)...66 (**78**, 90) sts.
5th rnd. K3 (**4**, 5), *sl 1, K1, psso, K1, K2tog, K6 (**8**, 10); rep from * to last 8 (**9**, 10) sts, sl 1, K1, psso, K1, K2tog, K3 (**4**, 5)...54 (**66**, 78) sts.
Cont dec in alt rnds in this manner, as *placed* in last 5 rnds, until the rnd "*sl 1, K1, psso, K1, K2tog, K1; rep from * to end...18 sts" has been worked.
Next rnd. Knit.
Next rnd. Slip first st to needle in right hand, *K1, K2tog; rep from * to end...12 sts.
Next rnd. *K2tog; rep from * to end...6 sts.
Knit 8 rnds on these 6 sts.
Break off yarn leaving a long thread. Thread yarn through these 6 sts, draw up and fasten off.

To make up

Using six strands DMC Stranded Cotton in colour/s as pictured, work a cross stitch on every alt st between dec at crown.

MOCCASINS

Beg at sole. Using 3.25mm needles, cast on 35 sts.
1st row (wrong side). Knit.
2nd row. K1, inc in next st, K14, inc in next st, K1, inc in next st, K14, inc in next st, K1...39 sts.
3rd and alt rows. Knit.
4th row. K1, inc in next st, K16, inc in next st, K1, inc in next st, K16, inc in next st, K1...43 sts.
6th row. K1, inc in next st, K18, inc in next st, K1, inc in next st, K18, inc in next st, K1...47 sts.
8th row. K1, inc in next st, K20, inc in next st, K1, inc in next st, K20, inc in next st, K1...51 sts.
9th row. Knit.
Work 5 rows st st.
Next row. Knit
Work 2 rows st st.
Shape for side of Moccasin. Next row. K16, K2tog, *turn*.
**Cont in st st on these 17 sts and dec one st at end of foll 4th rows until 14 sts rem.
Work one row.
Leave rem 14 sts on a stitch-holder.**
With right side facing, join yarn to rem 33 sts and K15, *turn*.
NOTE When *turning* (below), take yarn under needle and onto other side of work, slip next st onto righthand needle, take yarn under needle and back to original position, slip st back onto lefthand needle, then *turn* and proceed as instructed (this avoids making holes in work).
Shape toe. Cont on these 15 sts.
Next row. Purl to last st, *turn*.
Next row. Knit to last st, *turn*.
Next row. Purl to last 3 sts, *turn*.
Next row. Knit to last 3 sts, *turn*.
Next row. Purl to last 5 sts, *turn*.
Next row. Knit to last 5 sts, *turn*.
Next row. Purl to end.
Next row. K15.
Cont in st st on these 15 sts for tongue of Moccasin until work measures 8cm from purl ridge, ending with a purl row.
Cast off.
With right side facing, join yarn to rem 18 sts, K2tog, knit to end.
Rep from ** to **, noting to dec at beg instead of end.

EDGING

With right side facing and using 2.75mm needles, knit across 14 sts from stitch-holder at top of Moccasin, knit up 15 sts evenly along shaped edge, 13 sts evenly across top of toe of Moccasin where *turnings* were worked, 15 sts evenly along rem shaped edge, then knit across 14 sts from stitch-holder...71 sts.
Work 9 rows rev st st (purl fabric), beg with a knit row.
Cast off loosely.

To make up

Using six strands of DMC Stranded Cotton and colour/s as pictured, embroider in cross stitch rows 31 to 35 incl from Graph on page 105, between purl ridges, beg at centre st and working out to side edges. Join foot, heel, and back seam. Slipstitch tongue of Moccasin in position. Make a 25cm-long twisted cord and thread through Moccasin at ankle as pictured. Allow Edging (purl fabric) to roll to wrong side of Moccasin.

Cardigan, Hat and Bootees with Picot Edge and Bullion Roses

Page 40

Measurements

The three smallest sizes (A, ***B****, C) are to fit premature babies. The two larger sizes (D and E) are designed to fit 0-3 months (Size 000) and 3-6 months (Size 00).* ***Cardigan*** *to fit chest: 22 (****25****, 30,* ***35****, 40)cm; garment measures: 27 (****30****, 35,* ***40****, 45)cm; length: 16 (****18****, 20,* ***22****, 24)cm; sleeve length: approximately 6 (****7****, 9,* ***11****, 13)cm.* ***Hat*** *to fit head: approximately 21 (****25****, 30,* ***35****, 40)cm.* ***Bootees*** *to fit foot length: 4 (****5****, 6,* ***7****, 8)cm.*

Materials

Cleckheaton Baby Softwool 4-ply (25g):

- 2 (**2**, 3, **3**, 4) balls for **Cardigan**
- 1 (**1**, 1, **2**, 2) ball/s for **Hat**
- 1 ball (all sizes) for **Bootees**

or Cleckheaton Babysoft 4-ply (25g):

- 2 (**3**, 3, **4**, 4) balls for **Cardigan**
- 1 (**1**, 1, **2**, 2) ball/s for **Hat**
- 1 ball (all sizes) for **Bootees**

or Cleckheaton Lullaby 4-ply (75g):

- 1 (**1**, 1, **2**, 2) pullskein/s for **Cardigan**
- 1 pullskein (all sizes) for **Hat**
- 1 pullskein (all sizes) for **Bootees**
- One pair each 2.75mm (No 12), 3.25mm (No 10) and one set each of 2.75mm (No 12) and 3.25mm (No 10) knitting needles
- One skein DMC Stranded Embroidery Cotton in each of the three following colours: v. lt shell pink 224, pale dusty rose 963 and lt gumleaf green 3817
- Knitter's needle, for sewing seams and embroidery
- Three buttons

Tension

See **Knitting and Crochet Notes** on page 120.

28 sts and 36 rows to 10cm over st st, using 3.25mm needles.

CARDIGAN

BACK

Using 2.75mm needles, cast on 38 (**44**, 50, **58**, 64) sts.

Work 4 rows st st.

5th row (hemline). K1, *yfwd, K2tog, rep from * to last st, K1.

Change to 3.25mm needles.

Work 15 rows st st (beg with a purl row), inc one st in centre of last row...39 (**45**, 51, **59**, 65) sts.

Beg patt. 1st row. K4 (**7**, 0, **4**, 7), P1, *K9, P1, rep from * to last 4 (**7**, 0, **4**, 7) sts, K4, (**7**, 0, **4**, 7).

Work 11 rows st st, beg with a purl row.

13th row. K9 (**2**, 5, **9**, 2), P1, *K9, P1, rep from * to last 9 (**2**, 5, **9**, 2) sts, K9 (**2**, 5, **9**, 2).

Work 11 rows st st, beg with a purl row.

Last 24 rows form patt.

Cont in patt until work measures 16 (**18**, 20, **22**, 24)cm from hemline, working last row on wrong side.

Shape shoulders. Keeping patt correct, cast off 4 (**5**, 6, **7**, 7) sts at beg of next 4 rows, then 4 (**4**, 5, **6**, 8) sts at beg of foll 2 rows.

Cast off rem 15 (**17**, 17, **19**, 21) sts.

LEFT FRONT

Using 2.75mm needles, cast on 20 (**20**, 26, **30**, 30) sts.

Work 4 rows st st.

5th row (hemline). K1, *yfwd, K2tog, rep from * to last st, K1.

Change to 3.25mm needles.

Work 15 rows st st (beg with a purl row), dec (**inc**, dec, **dec**, inc) 1 (**2**, 1, **1**, 2) st/s evenly across last row...19 (**22**, 25, **29**, 32) sts.**

Beg patt. 1st row. K4 (**7**, 0, **4**, 7), P1, *K9, P1, rep from * to last 4 sts, K4.

Work 11 rows st st, beg with a purl row.

13th row. K0 (**2**, 5, **9**, 2), P0 (**1**, 1, **1**, 1), *K9, P1, rep from * to last 9 sts, K9.

Work 11 rows st st, beg with a purl row.

Last 24 rows form patt. Cont in patt until there are 9 (**9**, 13, **13**, 13) rows less than Back to beg of shoulder shaping, working last row on right side.

Shape neck. Keeping patt correct, cast off 3 (**4**, 4, **4**, 5) sts at beg of next row...16 (**18**, 21, **25**, 27) sts.

Dec one st at neck edge in next and foll alt row/s until 12 (**14**, 19, **21**, 23) sts rem, **Sizes C, D and E only**, then in foll 4th row/s until (17, **20**, 22) sts rem.

All sizes. Work 1 row patt.

Shape shoulder. Cast off 4 (**5**, 6, **7**, 7) sts at beg of next and foll alt row.

Work 1 row patt. Cast off rem 4 (**4**, 5, **6**, 8) sts.

RIGHT FRONT

Work as for Left Front to **.

Beg patt. 1st row. K4, P1, *K9, P1, rep from * to last 4 (**7**, 0, **4**, 7) sts, K4 (**7**, 0, **4**, 7).

Work 11 rows st st, beg with a purl row.

13th row. *K9, P1, rep from * to last 9 (**2**, 5, **9**, 2) sts, K9 (**2**, 5, **9**, 2).

Work 11 rows st st, beg with a purl row.

Last 24 rows form patt.

Cont in patt until there are 10 (**10**, 14, **14**, 14) rows less than Back to beg of shoulder shaping, working last row on wrong side.

Shape neck. Keeping patt correct, cast off 3 (**4**, 4, **4**, 5) sts at beg of next row...16 (**18**, 21, **25**, 27) sts.

Dec one st at neck edge in foll alt row/s until 12 (**14**, 19, **21**, 23) sts rem, **Sizes C, D and E only**, then in foll 4th row/s until 17 (**20**, 22) sts rem.

All sizes. Work 2 rows patt.

Shape shoulder. Work as given for Left Front shoulder shaping.

SLEEVES

Using 2.75mm needles, cast on 36 (**36**, 42, **48**, 48) sts.

Work 4 rows st st.

5th row (hemline). K1, *yfwd, K2tog, rep from * to last st, K1.

Change to 3.25mm needles.

Work 14 rows st st (beg with a purl row), *AT SAME TIME* inc one st at each end of 6th and foll 4th rows until there are 42 (**42**, 48, **54**, 54) sts.

Purl 1 row, dec one st in centre...41 (**41**, 47, **53**, 53) sts.

Beg patt. 1st row. K0 (**0**, 3, **1**, 1), P1, *K9, P1, rep from * to last 0 (**0**, 3, **1**, 1) st/s, K0 (**0**, 3, **1**, 1).

Sizes B, C, D and E only. Cont in patt as given for Back, as placed in last row, working extra sts into patt as they become available, inc one st at each end of 3rd and foll 4th row/s until there are (**45**, 53, **63**, 67) sts.

All sizes. Work 8 (**5**, 7, **7**, 5) rows patt (without further inc) on these 41 (**45**, 53, **63**, 67) sts.

Shape top. Keeping patt correct, cast off 5 (**5**, 6, **8**, 9) sts at beg of next 4 rows, then 5 (**6**, 7, **8**, 8) sts at beg of foll 2 rows. Cast off rem 11 (**13**, 15, **15**, 15) sts.

NECKBAND

Join shoulder seams. With right side facing and using 3.25mm needles, knit up 36 (**40**, 44, **48**, 52) sts evenly around neck edge.

Work 5 rows st st, beg with a purl row.

6th row (hemline). K1, *yfwd, K2tog, rep from * to last st, K1.

Change to 2.75mm needles.

Work 5 rows st st, beg with a purl row. Cast off **loosely**.

RIGHT FRONT BAND

Fold neckband and lower band in half at hemline onto wrong side and slipstitch **loosely** in position. With right side facing and using 3.25mm needles, knit up 32 (**38**, 40, **46**, 50) sts evenly along Right Front Edge, incl side edge of neckband (working through both thicknesses of lower band and neckband).

1st row (wrong side). Purl.

2nd row. K15 (**17**, 17, **21**, 21), [K2tog, yrn (to make a st), K4 (**6**, 7, **8**, 10)] twice, K2tog, yrn (to make a st), K3...3 buttonholes.

Work 3 rows st st, beg with a purl row.

6th row (hemline). K1, *yfwd, K2tog, rep from * to last st, K1.

Change to 2.75mm needles.

Work 5 rows st st, beg with a purl row and working buttonholes (as before) in 4th row. Cast off **loosely**.

LEFT FRONT BAND

Work as given for Right Front Band, omitting buttonholes.

To make up

Tie a marker 8 (**9**, 10, **11**, 12)cm down from beg of shoulder shaping on side edges of Back and Fronts to mark armholes. Placing centre of Sleeves to shoulder seams, sew in Sleeves evenly between markers. Join side and sleeve seams. Fold lower edge, Sleeve edges and Front Bands at hemline onto wrong side and slipstitch loosely in position. Using three strands DMC Stranded Cotton and following the diagram, below, work flowers as photographed, working flowers in bullion stitch, stems in stem stitch and leaves in lazy daisy stitch (see **Embroidery Stitch Guide** on page 112). Sew on buttons.

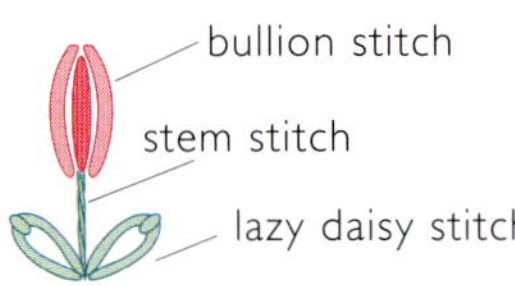

HAT

Using set of 2.75mm needles, cast on 60 (**70**, 80, **100**, 110) sts evenly onto 3 needles.

1st rnd. Purl

Rep first rnd 4 times (5 rnds in all).

6th rnd (hemline). *P2tog, yrn (to make a st), rep from * to end.

Change to set of 3.25mm needles.

Purl 1 (**1**, 3, **5**, 5) rnd/s.

Next rnd. *P9, K1, rep from * to end.

Purl 11 rnds.

Next rnd. P4, *K1, P9, rep from * to last 6 sts, K1, P5.

Purl 0 (**0**, 2, **4**, 4) rnds.

Next rnd. *K1, P1, rep from * to end.

Rep last rnd 7 (**9**, 11, **13**, 13) times.

Knit 21 (**22**, 24, **26**, 27) rnds.

Shape crown. 1st rnd. *K2tog, K5, sl 1, K1, psso, K1, rep from * to end...48 (**56**, 64, **80**, 88) sts.

Knit 2 rnds.

4th rnd. *K2tog, K3, sl 1, K1, psso, K1, rep from * to end...36 (**42**, 48, **60**, 66) sts.

Knit 2 rnds.

7th rnd. *K2tog, K1, sl 1, K1, psso, K1, rep from * to end...24 (**28**, 32, **40**, 44) sts.

Knit 2 rnds.

10th rnd. *K3tog, K1, rep from * to end...12 (**14**, 16, **20**, 22) sts.

13th rnd. *K2tog, rep from * to end...6 (**7**, 8, **10**, 11) sts.

Break off yarn, run end through rem sts, draw up and fasten off securely.

To make up

Fold Picot edge onto wrong side at hemline and slipstitch **loosely** in position. Fold band onto right side. Embroider flowers as given for **Cardigan**, using photograph as a guide to placement.

BOOTEES (make 2; beg at ankle)

Using 2.75mm needles, **loosely** cast on 26 (**28**, 32, **34**, 38) sts.

Work 4 rows st st.

5th row (hemline). K1, *yfwd, K2tog, rep from * to last st, K1.

Change to 3.25mm needles.

Work 3 (**3**, 5, **5**, 7) rows st st (beg with a purl row), inc one st in centre of first row...27 (**29**, 33, **35**, 39) sts.

Beg Main Patt. 1st row. K8 (**9**, 1, **2**, 4), P1, *K9, P1, rep from * to last 8 (**9**, 1, **2**, 4) st/s, K8 (**9**, 1, **2**, 4).

Work 11 rows st st, beg with a purl row.

Next row. K3 (**4**, 6, **7**, 9), P1, *K9, P1, rep from * to last 3 (**4**, 6, **7**, 9) sts, K3 (**4**, 6, **7**, 9).

Shape for instep. Next row. P17 (**18**, 20, **21**, 23), *turn*, K7, *turn*.

Cont on centre 7 sts (leaving 10 (**11**, 13, **14**, 16) sts on needle at each end) and work 9 (**11**, 13, **15**, 17) rows st st, beg with a purl row. *Turn*, break off yarn and leaves these 7 sts on lefthand needle.

Shape sides. With right side facing, rejoin yarn to end of 10 (**11**, 13, **14**, 16) sts at right edge, knit up 7 (**9**, 11, **13**, 15) sts evenly along first side of instep, knit across 7 sts from centre, then knit up 7 (**9**, 11, **13**, 15) sts evenly along 2nd side of instep, then knit across rem 10 (**11**, 13, **14**, 16) sts...41 (**47**, 55, **61**, 69) sts.

Work 3 (**5**, 7, **9**, 11) rows st st, beg with a purl row.

Shape heel and toe. 1st row. K2tog, K16 (**19**, 23, **26**, 30), K2tog, K1, K2tog, K16 (**19**, 23, **26**, 30), K2tog...37 (**43**, 51, **57**, 65) sts.

2nd row. Purl.

3rd row. K2tog, K14 (**17**, 21, **24**, 28), K2tog, K1, K2tog, K14 (**17**, 21, **24**, 28), K2tog...33 (**39**, 47, **53**, 61) sts.

4th row. P2tog, P12 (**15**, 19, **22**, 26), P2tog, P1, P2tog, P12 (**15**, 19, **22**, 26), P2tog...29 (**35**, 43, **49**, 57) sts.

5th row. K2tog, K10 (**13**, 17, **20**, 24), K2tog, K1, K2tog, K10 (**13**, 17, **20**, 24), K2tog...25 (**31**, 39, **45**, 53) sts.

6th row. P2tog, P9 (**12**, 16, **19**, 23), P3tog, P9 (**12**, 16, **19**, 23), P2tog...21 (**27**, 35, **41**, 49) sts.

Work 2 rows st st. Cast off **loosely**.

To make up

Join back and foot seam. Fold Picot edge in half at hemline and slipstitch **loosely** in position. Embroider flowers as given for **Cardigan**, using the photograph as a guide to placement.

Cardigan, Hat and Bootees in 8-ply Garter Stitch

Page 41

Measurements

The three smallest sizes (A, B, C) are to fit premature babies. The two larger sizes (D and E) are designed to fit 0-3 months (Size 000) and 3-6 months (Size 00). ***Cardigan*** *to fit chest: 22 (**25**, 30, **35**, 40)cm; garment measures: 27 (**30**, 35, **40**, 45)cm; length: 16 (**17**, 20, **22**, 24)cm; sleeve length: approximately 6 (**7**, 9, **11**, 13)cm.* ***Hat*** *to fit head: approximately 21 (**25**, 30, **35**, 40)cm.* ***Bootees*** *to fit foot length: 4 (**5**, 6, **7**, 8)cm.*

Materials

Cleckheaton Cotton/Wool 8-ply (50g):
- 2 (**2**, 2, **3**, 3) balls for **Cardigan**
- 1 ball (all sizes) for **Hat**
- 1 ball (all sizes) for **Bootees**

or Cleckheaton Country 8-ply (50g):
- 2 (**2**, 2, **3**, 3) balls for **Cardigan**
- 1 ball (all sizes) for **Hat**
- 1 ball (all sizes) for **Bootees**

or Cleckheaton Courtelle 8-ply (100g):
- 1 ball (all sizes) for **Cardigan**
- 1 ball (all sizes) for **Hat**
- 1 ball (all sizes) for **Bootees**

or Cleckheaton Machinewash 8-ply (50g):
- 2 (**2**, 2, **3**, 3) balls for **Cardigan**
- 1 ball (all sizes) for **Hat**
- 1 ball (all sizes) for **Bootees**
- One pair 4.00mm (No 8) and one set 4.00mm (No 8) knitting needles
- Knitter's needle, for sewing seams
- Three buttons

Tension

See **Knitting and Crochet Notes** on page 120.
21 sts and 44 rows to 10cm over garter st, using 4.00mm needles.

CARDIGAN

BACK

Using 4.00mm needles, cast on 31 (**33**, 39, **45**, 49) sts.
Work in garter st until work measures 16 (**17**, 20, **22**, 24)cm from beg, working last row on wrong side.
Shape shoulders. Cast off 3 (**3**, 4, **5**, 6) sts at beg of next 4 rows, then 4 (**4**, 5, **5**, 5) sts at beg of foll 2 rows. Cast off rem 11 (**13**, 13, **15**, 15) sts.

LEFT FRONT

Using 4.00mm needles, cast on 15 (**16**, 19, **22**, 24) sts.
Work as given for Back until there are 11 (**13**, 13, **17**, 17) rows less than Back to beg of shoulder shaping, working last row on right side.
Shape neck. Cast off 2 (**3**, 3, **3**, 3) sts at beg of next row...13 (**13**, 16, **19**, 21) sts.
Dec one st at neck edge in next and foll 4th rows until 10 (10**, 13, **15**, 17) sts rem.
Work 1 (**3**, 3, **3**, 3) row/s garter st.**
Shape shoulder. Cast off 3 (**3**, 4, **5**, 6) sts at beg of next and foll alt row.
Knit 1 row.
Cast off rem 4 (**4**, 5, **5**, 5) sts.

RIGHT FRONT

Using 4.00mm needles, cast on 15 (**16**, 19, **22**, 24) sts.
Work as given for Back until there are 12 (**14**, 14, **18**, 18) rows less than Back to beg of shoulder shaping, working last row on wrong side.
Shape neck. Cast off 2 (**3**, 3, **3**, 3) sts at beg of next row...13 (**13**, 16, **19**, 21) sts.
Knit 1 row.
Work as given for Left Front from ** to **.
Knit 1 row.
Shape shoulder. Work as given for Left Front shoulder shaping.

SLEEVES

Using 4.00mm needles, cast on 23 (**27**, 29, **31**, 33) sts.
Work in garter st, inc one st at each end of 4th and foll 8th (**10th**, 10th, **8th**, 8th) rows until there are 29 (**33**, 37, **41**, 47) sts.
Cont (without further inc) until work measures 6 (**7**, 9, **11**, 13)cm from beg, working last row on wrong side.
Shape top. Cast off 3 (**4**, 5, **5**, 6) sts at beg of next 4 rows, then 4 (**4**, 4, **5**, 6) sts at beg of foll 2 rows. Cast off rem 9 (**9**, 9, **11**, 11) sts.

NECKBAND

Join shoulder seams. With right side facing and using 4.00mm needles, knit up 35 (**41**, 41, **47**, 47) sts evenly around neck edge. Knit 1 row.
Cast off **loosely**.

LEFT FRONT BAND

With right side facing, using 4.00mm needles and beg at neck edge of Left Front, knit up 2 sts, yfwd (to make a buttonhole), miss 2 rows, *knit up 4 (**5**, 6, **7**, 8) sts, yfwd (to make a buttonhole), miss 2 rows, rep from * once, knit up 10 (**10**, 16, **20**, 24) sts evenly along rem of Left Front edge...26 (**28**, 36, **42**, 48) sts (counting each yfwd as 2 sts)...3 buttonholes.
Knit 1 row, (knitting into front and back of each yfwd).
Cast off **loosely.**

RIGHT FRONT BAND

Work as given for Left Front Band, omitting buttonholes.

To make up

Tie a marker 8 (**9**, 10, **11**, 12)cm down from beg of shoulder shaping on side edges of Back and Fronts to mark armholes. Placing centre of Sleeves to shoulder seams, sew in Sleeves evenly between markers. Join side and Sleeve seams. Sew on buttons.

HAT

Using set of 4.00mm needles, cast on 42 (**48**, 54, **66**, 78) sts evenly onto 3 needles.
1st rnd. Purl
2nd rnd. Knit.
Rep last 2 rnds 7 (**8**, 9, **11**, 12) times...16 (**18**, 20, **24**, 26) rnds in all.
Purl 3 rnds (for hemline of band).
Rep first 2 rnds 11 (**14**, 16, **19**, 21) times...22 (**28**, 32, **38**, 42) rnds in all.
Purl 1 rnd.
Shape crown. 1st rnd. *Sl 1, K1, psso, K1, K2tog, K2 (**3**, 4, **6**, 8), rep from * to end...30 (**36**, 42, **54**, 66) sts.
2nd and alt rnds. Purl.
3rd rnd. *Sl 1, K1, psso, K1, K2tog, K0 (**1**, 2, **4**, 6), rep from * to end...18 (**24**, 30, **42**, 54) sts.

Sizes C, D and E only. Cont dec in alt rnd/s in this manner, as placed in last 3 rnds, until the rnd "*Sl 1, K1, psso, K1, K2tog, rep from * to end…18 sts" has been worked.

All Sizes. Next rnd. Purl.

Next rnd. Slip first st to needle in right hand, *K1, K2tog, rep from * to end…12 (**16**, 12, **12**, 12) sts.

Next rnd. *K2tog. rep from * to end...6 (**8**, 6, **6**, 6) sts.

Break off yarn, run end through rem sts and fasten off securely. Fold band onto right side.

BOOTEES (make 2; beg at ankle)

Using 4.00mm needles, cast on 20 (**22**, 24, **26**, 28) sts.

Work 13 (**15**, 17, **19**, 21) rows garter st (1st row is wrong side).

Shape for instep. Next row. K12 (**13**, 15, **16**, 17), *turn*, K4 (**4**, 6, **6**, 6), *turn*.

Cont on centre 4 (**4**, 6, **6**, 6) sts [leaving 8 (**9**, 9, **10**, 11) sts on needle at each end] and work 10 (**12**, 14, **16**, 18) rows garter st. *Turn*, break off yarn and leave these 4 (**4**, 6, **6**, 6) sts on lefthand needle.

Shape sides. With right side facing, rejoin yarn to end of 8 (**9**, 9, **10**, 11) sts at right edge, knit up 6 (**7**, 8, **9**, 10) sts evenly along first side of instep, knit across 4 (**4**, 6, **6**, 6) sts from centre of instep, knit up 6 (**7**, 8, **9**, 10) sts evenly along 2nd side of instep, then knit across rem 8 (**9**, 9, **10**, 11) sts…32 (**36**, 40, **44**, 48) sts.

Work 5 (**5**, 7, **9**, 11) rows garter st.

Shape heel and toe. 1st row. K2tog, K12 (**14**, 16, **18**, 20), (K2tog) twice, K12 (**14**, 16, **18**, 20), K2tog…28 (**32**, 36, **40**, 44) sts.

2nd and alt rows. Knit.

3rd row. K2tog, K10 (**12**, 14, **16**, 18), (K2tog) twice, K10 (**12**, 14, **16**, 18), K2tog…24 (**28**, 32, **36**, 40) sts.

5th row. K2tog, K8 (**10**, 12, **14**, 16), (K2tog) twice, K8 (**10**, 12, **14**, 16), K2tog…20 (**24**, 28, **32**, 36) sts.

Knit 1 row.

Cast off **loosely.**

To make up

Join back and foot seam.

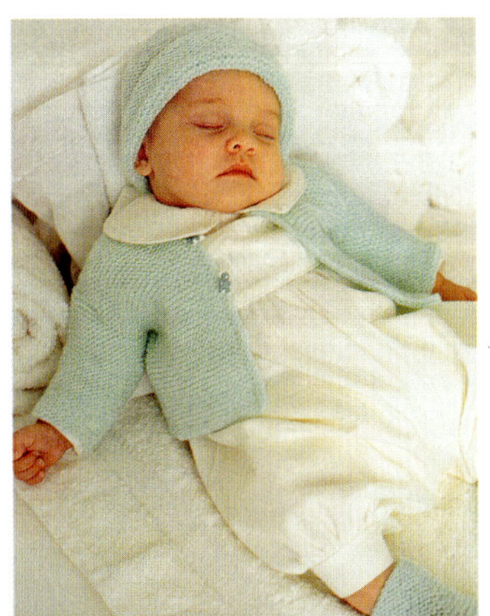

Cardigan, Hat and Bootees in 4-ply Garter Stitch

Page 41

Measurements

The three smallest sizes (A, B, C) are to fit premature babies. The two larger sizes (D and E) are designed to fit 0-3 months (Size 000) and 3-6 months (Size 00). ***Cardigan*** *to fit chest: 22 (**25**, 30, **35**, 40)cm; garment measures: 27 (**30**, 35, **40**, 45)cm; length: 16 (**17**, 20, **22**, 24)cm; sleeve length: approximately 6 (**7**, 9, **11**, 13)cm.* ***Hat*** *to fit head: approximately 21 (**25**, 30, **35**, 40)cm.* ***Bootees*** *to fit foot length: 4 (**5**, 6, **7**, 8)cm.*

Materials

Cleckheaton Baby Softwool 4-ply (25g):

- 2 (**2**, 3, **4**, 4) balls for **Cardigan**
- 1 (**1**, 1, **2**, 2) ball/s for **Hat**
- 1 ball (all sizes) for **Bootees**

or Cleckheaton Babysoft 4-ply (25g):

- 2 (**2**, 3, **4**, 4) balls for **Cardigan**
- 1 (**1**, 1, **2**, 2) ball/s for **Hat**
- 1 ball (all sizes) for **Bootees**

or Cleckheaton Lullaby 4-ply (75g):

- 1 (**1**, 1, **2**, 2) pullskein/s for **Cardigan**
- 1 pullskein (all sizes) for **Hat**
- 1 pullskein (all sizes) for **Bootees**
- One pair each 3.00mm (No 11), 3.25mm (No 10) and one set of 3.25mm (No 10) knitting needles
- Knitter's needle, for sewing seams
- Three buttons

Tension

See **Knitting and Crochet Notes** on page 120. 25 sts and 52 rows to 10cm over garter st, using 3.25mm needles.

CARDIGAN

BACK

Using 3.25mm needles, cast on 35 (**39**, 45, **53**, 59) sts.

Work in garter st until work measures 16 (**17**, 20, **22**, 24)cm from beg, working last row on wrong side.

Shape shoulders. Cast off 4 (**4**, 5, **6**, 7) sts at beg of next 4 rows, then 3 (**4**, 4, **5**, 6) sts at beg of foll 2 rows. Cast off rem 13 (**15**, 17, **19**, 19) sts.

LEFT FRONT

Using 3.25mm needles, cast on 17 (**19**, 22, **26**, 29) sts.

Work as given for Back until there are 13 (**15**, 15, **19**, 19) rows less than Back to beg of shoulder shaping, working last row on right side.

Shape neck. Cast off 3 (**3**, 4, **4**, 4) sts at beg of next row…14 (**16**, 18, **22**, 25) sts.

Dec one st at neck edge in next and foll 4th rows until 11 (12**, 14, **17**, 20) sts rem.

Work 3 (**1**, 1, **1**, 1) row/s garter st.**

Shape shoulder. Cast off 4 (**4**, 5, **6**, 7) sts at beg of next and foll alt row.

Knit 1 row.

Cast off rem 3 (**4**, 4, **5**, 6) sts.

RIGHT FRONT

Using 3.25mm needles, cast on 17 (**19**, 22, **26**, 29) sts.

Work as given for Back until there are 14 (**16**, 16, **20**, 20) rows less than Back to beg of shoulder shaping, working last row on wrong side.

Shape neck. Cast off 3 (**3**, 4, **4**, 4) sts at beg of next row…14 (**16**, 18, **22**, 25) sts.

Knit 1 row.

Work as given for Left Front from ** to **.

Knit 1 row.

Shape shoulder. Work as given for Left Front shoulder shaping.

SLEEVES

Using 3.25mm needles, cast on 29 (**31**, 33, **35**, 39) sts.

Work in garter st, inc one st at each end of 4th and foll 10th (**8th**, 6th, **8th**, 8th) rows until there are 35 (**39**, 45, **49**, 55) sts.

Cont (without further inc) until work measures 6 (**7**, 9, **11**, 13)cm from beg, working last row on wrong side.

Shape top. Cast off 4 (**5**, 6, **6**, 7) sts at beg of next 4 rows, then 5 (**5**, 5, **6**, 7) sts at beg of foll 2 rows. Cast off rem 9 (**9**, 11, **13**, 13) sts.

NECKBAND

Join shoulder seams. With right side facing and using 3.00mm needles, knit up 34 (**40**, 44, **48**, 48) sts evenly around neck edge. Knit 1 row. Cast off **loosely**.

LEFT FRONT BAND

With right side facing, using 3.00mm needles and beg at neck edge of Left Front, knit up 2 sts, yfwd, miss 2 rows (to make a buttonhole), *knit up 5 (**6**, 7, **8**, 9) sts, yfwd, miss 2 rows (to make a buttonhole), rep from * once, knit up 12 (**14**, 16, **20**, 22) sts evenly along rem of Left Front edge…30 (**34**, 38, **44**, 48) sts (counting each yfwd as 2 sts)…3 buttonholes.

Knit 1 row, (knitting into front and back of each yfwd).

Cast off **loosely**.

RIGHT FRONT BAND

Work as given for Left Front Band, omitting buttonholes.

To make up

Tie a marker 8 (**9**, 10, **11**, 12)cm down from beg of shoulder shaping on side edges of Back and Fronts to mark armholes. Placing centre of Sleeves to shoulder seams, sew in Sleeves evenly between markers. Join side and Sleeve seams. Sew on buttons.

HAT

Using set of 3.25mm needles, cast on 48 (**60**, 72, **84**, 96) sts evenly onto 3 needles.
1st rnd. Purl
2nd rnd. Knit.
Rep last 2 rnds 8 (**9**, 11, **13**, 14) times...18 (**20**, 24, **28**, 30) rnds in all.
Purl 3 rnds (for hemline of band).
Rep first 2 rnds 12 (**15**, 18, **20**, 23) times...24 (**30**, 36, **40**, 46) rnds in all.
Purl 1 rnd.
Shape crown. 1st rnd. *Sl 1, K1, psso, K1, K2tog, K3 (**5**, 7, **9**, 11), rep from * to end...36 (**48**, 60, **72**, 84) sts.
2nd and alt rnds. Purl.
3rd rnd. *Sl 1, K1, psso, K1, K2tog, K1 (**3**, 5, **7**, 9), rep from * to end...24 (**36**, 48, **60**, 72) sts.
Cont dec in alt rnd/s in this manner, as placed in last 3 rnds, until 12 sts rem.
Next rnd. Purl.
Next rnd. *K2tog. rep from * to end...6 sts.
Break off yarn, run end through rem sts, draw up and fasten off securely. Fold band onto right side.

BOOTEES (make 2; beg at ankle)

Using 3.25mm needles, cast on 22 (**24**, 26, **28**, 30) sts.
Work 17 (**19**, 21, **23**, 25) rows garter st (1st row is wrong side).
Shape for instep. Next row. K14 (**15**, 16, **17**, 18), *turn*, K6, *turn*.
Cont on centre 6 sts [leaving 8 (**9**, 10, **11**, 12) sts on needle at each end] and work 12 (**14**, 16, **18**, 20) rows garter st.
Shape sides. With right side facing, rejoin yarn to end of 8 (**9**, 10, **11**, 12) sts at right edge, knit up 7 (**8**, 9, **10**, 11) sts evenly along first side of instep, knit across 6 sts from centre of instep, knit up 7 (**8**, 9, **10**, 11) sts evenly along 2nd side of instep, then knit across rem 8 (**9**, 10, **11**, 12) sts...36 (**40**, 44, **48**, 52) sts.
Work 7 (**9**, 11, **13**, 15) rows garter st.
Shape heel and toe. 1st row. K2tog, K14 (**16**, 18, **20**, 22), (K2tog) twice, K14 (**16**, 18, **20**, 22), K2tog...32 (**36**, 40, **44**, 48) sts.
2nd and alt rows. Knit.
3rd row. K2tog, K12 (**14**, 16, **18**, 20), (K2tog) twice, K12 (**14**, 16, **18**, 20), K2tog...28 (**32**, 36, 40, **44**) sts.
5th row. K2tog, K10 (**12**, 14, **16**, 18), (K2tog) twice, K10 (**12**, 14, **16**, 18), K2tog...24 (**28**, 32, **36**, 40) sts.
Knit 1 row.
Cast off **loosely**.

To make up

Join back and foot seam.

Knitted Bunny

Page 64

Measurements

Finished Bunny is 15-19cm tall.

Materials

Patons Dream Time Baby Wool 4-ply (25g):

- 1 ball
- One pair 3.00mm (No 11) needles
- Knitter's needle for sewing seams
- Polyester fibrefill
- Wool or stranded cotton, for features (optional)
- Narrow ribbon, for neck (optional)

Tension

See **Knitting and Crochet Notes** on page 120.
31 sts to 10cm in width over garter st.

LEG/BODY (make 2)

Using 3.00mm needles, cast on 12 sts.
Knit 2 rows garter st.
3rd row. *Inc in next st, K1; rep from * to end...18 sts.
Knit 21 rows garter st.
Tie a coloured thread at each end of last row to mark top of leg.
Knit a further 22 rows garter st.
47th and 48th rows. *K1, K2tog; rep from * to end...8 sts.
Cast off.

RIGHT HEAD

Using 3.00mm needles, cast on 11 sts.
1st row. Knit.
Cont in garter st, inc at end of next row and at same edge in every row until there are 18 sts.
Knit 1 row.
Dec at shaped edge in every row until 14 sts rem.
Dec at each end of next row and foll alt row...10 sts.
Cast off.

LEFT HEAD

Using 3.00mm needles, cast on 11 sts.
1st row. Knit.
Cont in garter st, inc at beg of next row and at same edge in every row until there are 18 sts.
Knit 1 row.
Dec at shaped edge in every row until 14 sts rem.
Dec at each end of next row and foll alt row...10 sts.
Cast off.

EAR (make 4)

Using 3.00mm needles, cast on 8 sts.
Knit 20 rows garter st.
Dec at each end of next and alt rows until 2 sts rem.
Next row. K2, *turn*, K2tog.
Fasten off.

ARM (make 2)

Using 3.00mm needles, cast on 10 sts.
Knit 2 rows garter st.
3rd row. *Inc in next st, K1; rep from * to end...15 sts.
Knit 15 rows garter st.
19th row. K1, *K2tog; rep from * to end...8 sts.
Knit 1 row.
Cast off.

TAIL

Using 3.00mm needles, cast on 4 sts.
Knit in garter st, inc at each end of alt rows until there are 10 sts.
Knit 5 rows garter st.
Dec at each end of next and alt rows until 4 sts rem.
Cast off.

To make up

Fold one Body piece in half lengthwise, right sides tog. Using backstitch, sew foot seam across cast-on edge, then join Leg seam to coloured threads. Repeat for second Body piece. With right sides tog, push one Leg inside the other and stitch centre/front back seam, matching inside Leg seams. Turn right side out and stuff lightly. Run a gathering thread around open upper edge, pull up thread tightly and fasten off.

With right sides tog and using backstitch, join Head sections, leaving cast-on edge (neck edge) open. Turn right side out, fill lightly, then stitch Head firmly to top of Body.

With right sides tog and using backstitch, join Ears tog in pairs, leaving straight cast-on edge open. Turn right side out. Fold a pleat in the straight edge, then stitch Ears firmly to Head, as photographed.

Fold each Arm piece in half lengthwise, right sides together. Using backstitch, join seams, leaving cast-off edge open. Turn right side out, fill lightly and sew Arms firmly to Body.

Run a gathering thread around edge of Tail, draw up tightly and fasten off. Stitch Tail firmly to lower back of Body.

If desired, using wool or stranded cotton, embroider simple facial features – eyes, nose and mouth.

Tie a ribbon around Bunny's neck, if desired, but remember to stitch it firmly in place to avoid its becoming a choking hazard.

Embroidery Stitch Guide

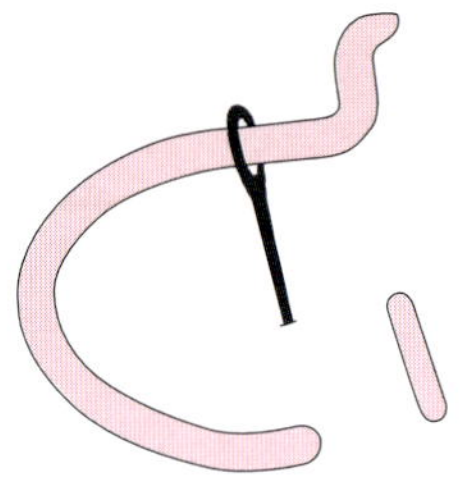
straight stitch

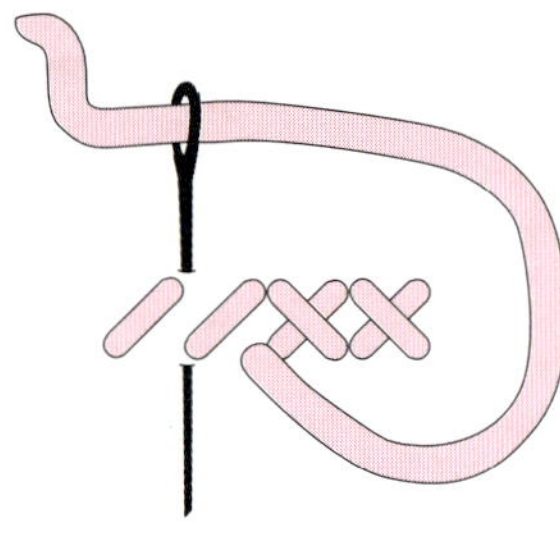
cross stitch

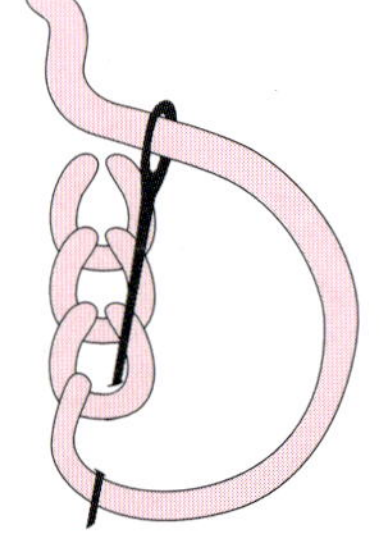
chain stitch

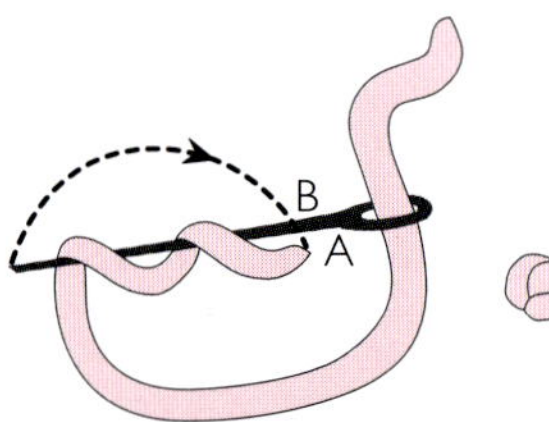

French knot

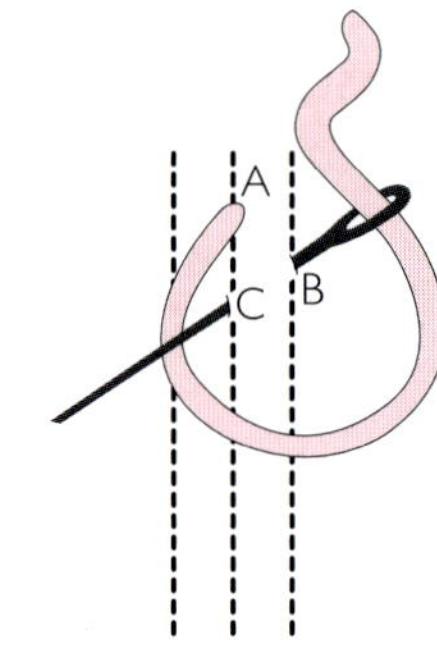

feather stitch

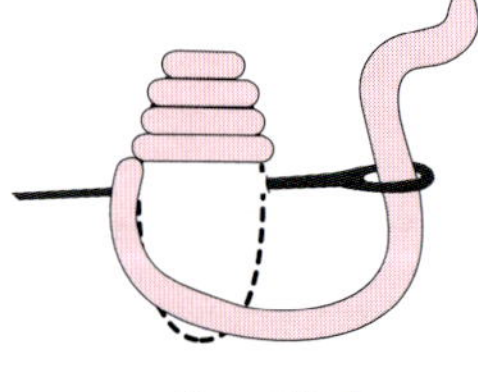
satin stitch

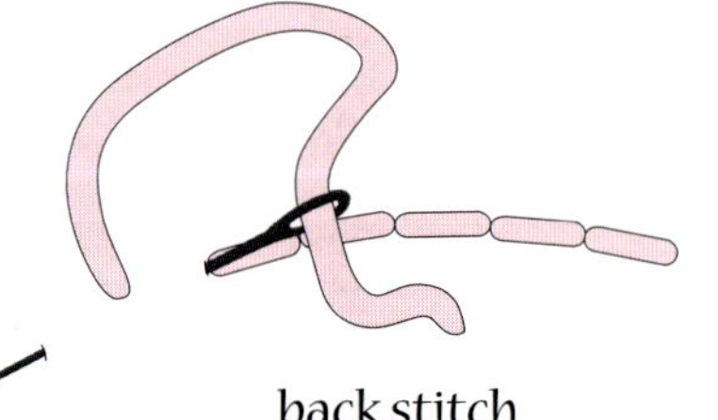
back stitch

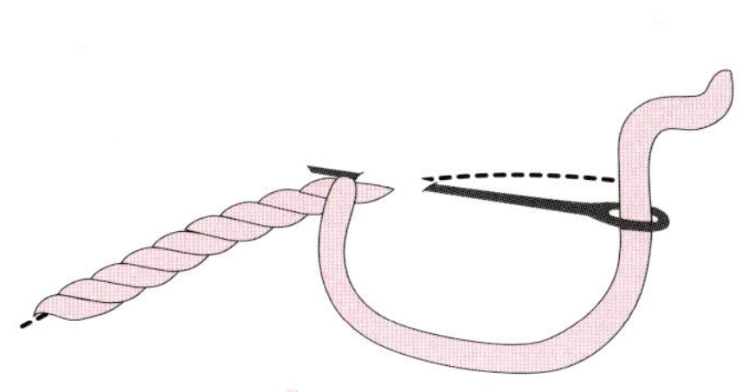

stem stitch

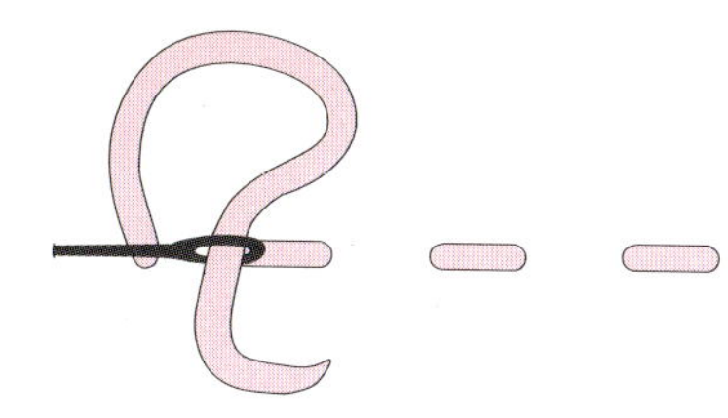

running stitch

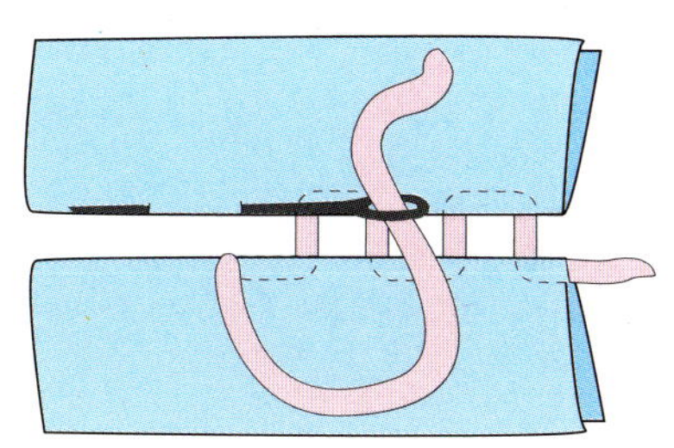

fly stitch

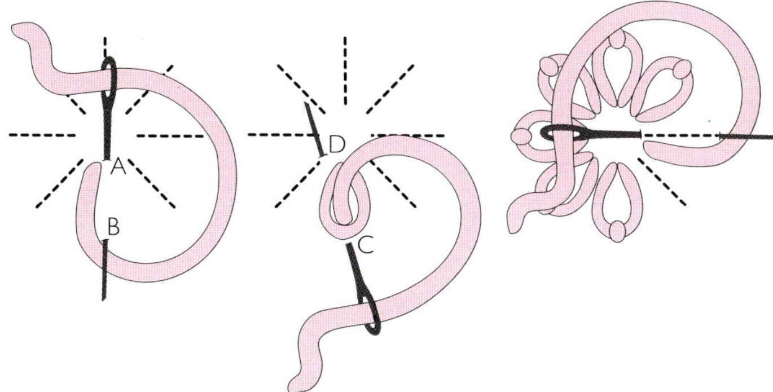

lazy daisy stitch

ladder stitch

basketweave stitch

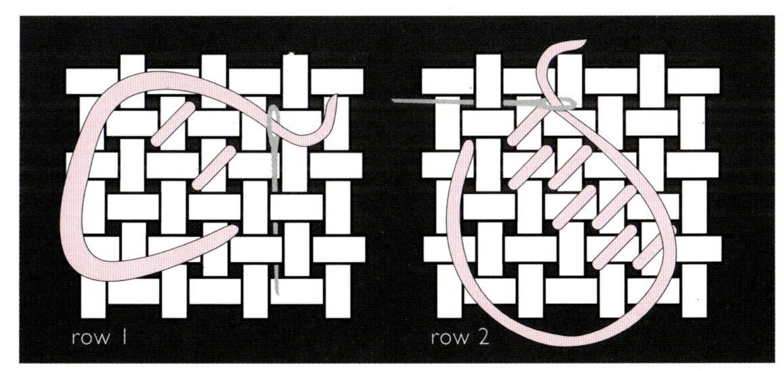

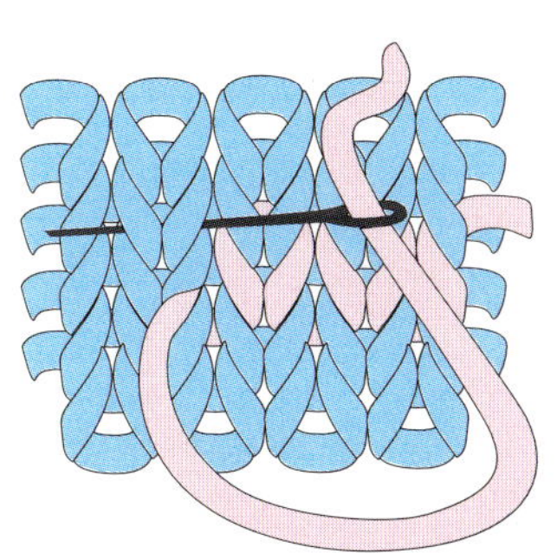

knitting stitch

tent stitch

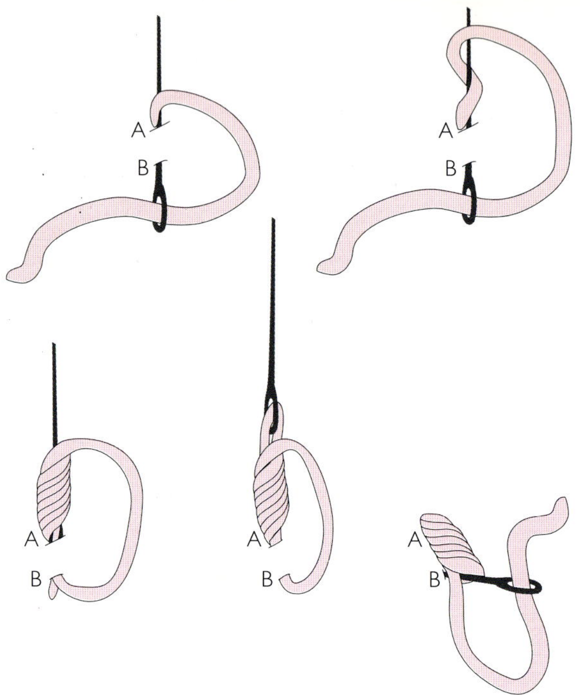

bullion stitch

Bring needle up at A and insert it at B, about 3mm from A, bringing half the length of needle, out again at A. Wrap thread around needle up to eight times, to fill length of stitch (A–B). Holding the coils of thread with one hand, pull the needle and thread carefully through the coils, then ease the coils along the thread with the needle so they fill the length of the stitch. Insert the needle into the fabric at B and bring it up in position for the next stitch.

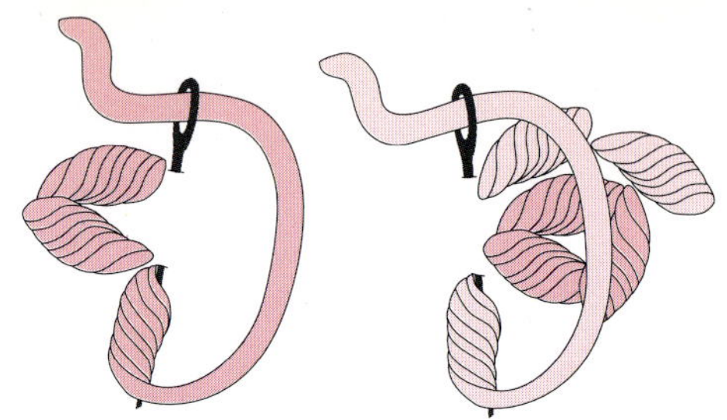

bullion stitch rose

To work a bullion stitch rose, use the darkest shade of thread (say, deep pink) to embroider three bullion stitches in a triangle, for the centre of the rose. Change to a lighter shade of pink and work 5–7 more bullion stitches around the original triangle, overlapping them slightly. If desired, another round of bullion stitches in an even paler pink can be added, to produce a larger rose.

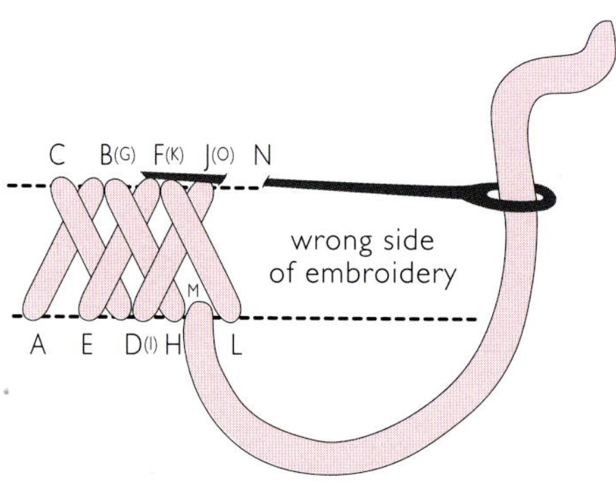

shadow stitch

Shadow stitch is a close herringbone stitch worked on the wrong side of sheer fabric. Transfer outline to wrong side of fabric. Bring needle up at A, insert at B, take a small horizontal back stitch and re-emerge at C. Take needle back down to D and take a back stitch to re-emerge at E. Take needle up to F and take a back stitch to re-emerge in the same hole as B. Fill in outline of design with herringbone stitch, taking care not to leave gaps between back stitches on the right side. Where there is a curve in the design, work smaller stitches on the inside of a curve and longer stitches on the outside edge, to maintain continuity in the herringbone.

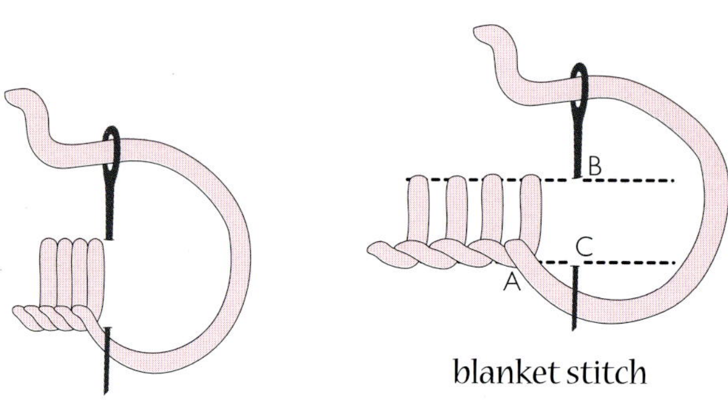

buttonhole stitch

blanket stitch

shell stitch

Stitching along the folded edge of fabric, take a blanket stitch to form a loop. Before stitch is pulled tight, work three buttonhole stitches into the loop, pulling them together to form a 'shell'. Repeat to form shell stitch border.

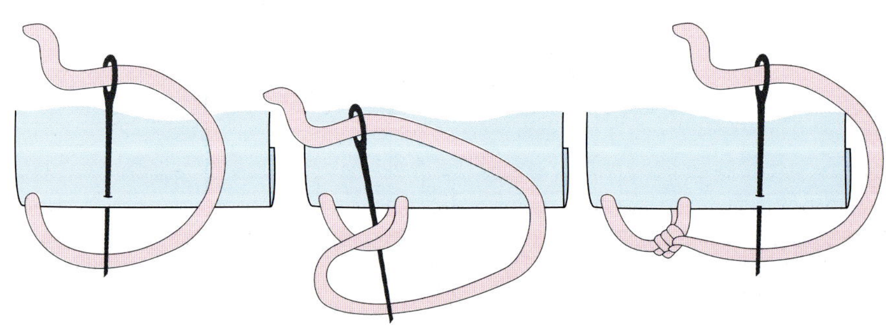

Wool Embroidery Stitch Guide

Small daisy

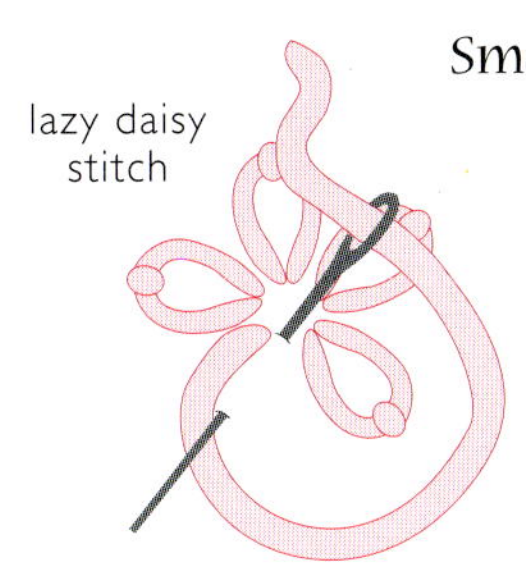

Ribbon and Bow

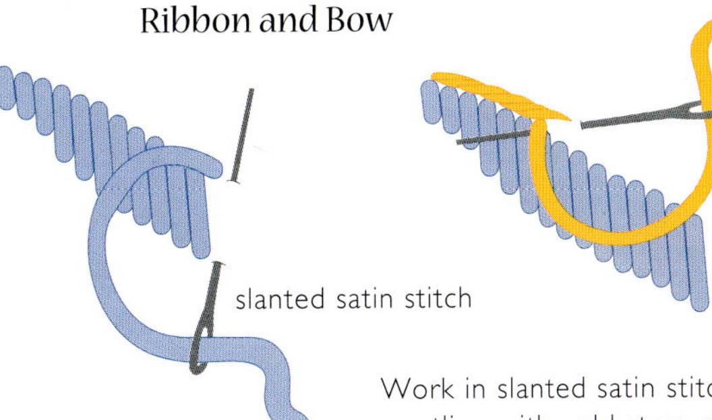

Work in slanted satin stitch and outline with gold stem stitch.

Large daisy

Work a straight stitch in the centre of each lazy daisy petal, and a group of French knots at centre. Fly stitch can be added to points of random flowers, for extra colour.

fly stitch

Lavender

Work lazy daisy flowers and stem stitch stems. Add random green straight stitches for leaves.

Winter rose

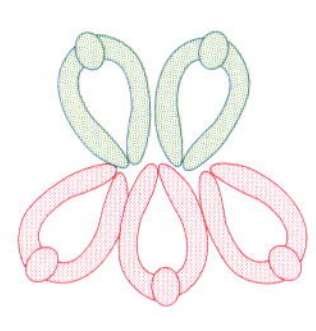

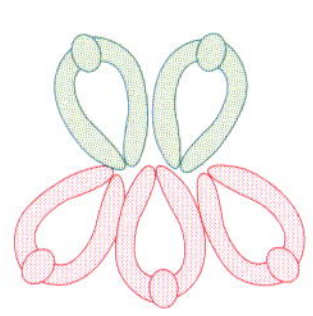

Work three pink lazy daisy stitches from the same hole, fanning downwards, and two green smaller lazy daisy stitches from the same hole, pointing upwards.

Forget-me-not

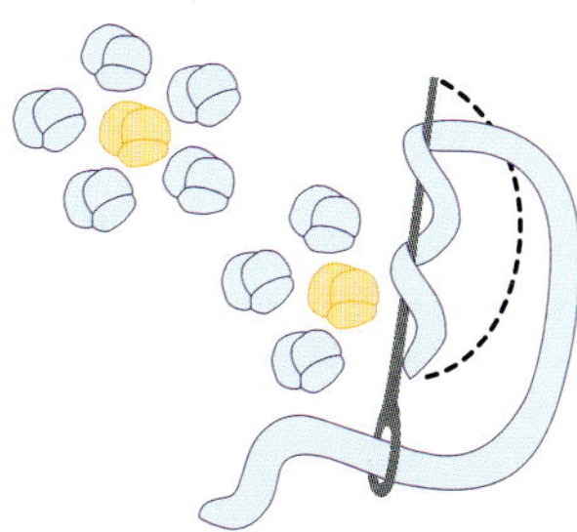

Work five blue French knots, with a yellow knot at centre.

Graphs for Quick Cross Stitch

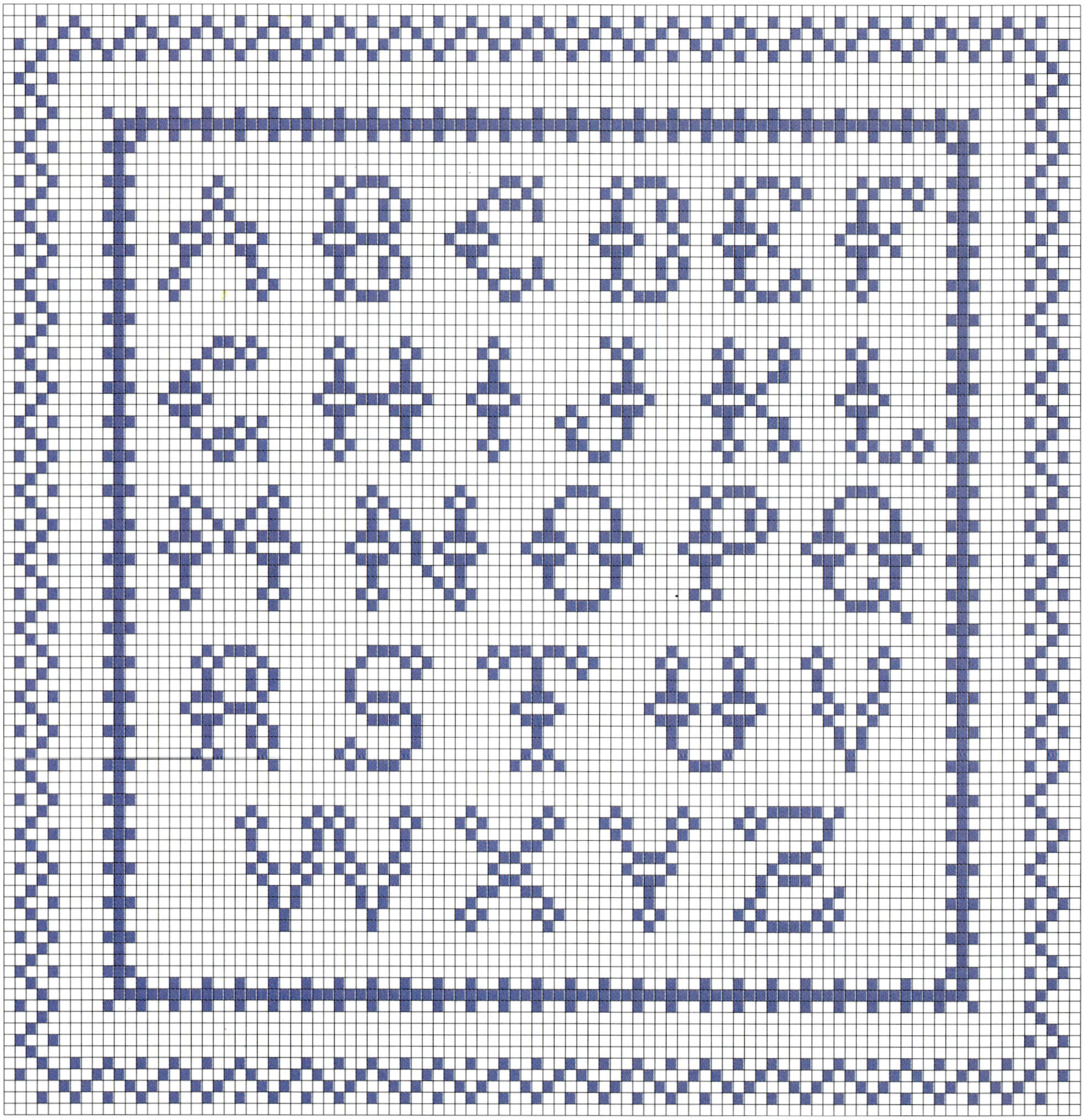

Basic Appliqué Techniques

All appliqué outlines are printed actual size on the pattern sheet. Place double-sided appliqué webbing, paper side up, over desired outline (it should show through easily) and use a fine marker or pencil to trace directly onto webbing. Note that a reverse image results from tracing. If you want your motif to face the same way as it is printed, you will need to trace it onto tracing paper first, then turn the tracing over (so that image is reversed) and trace it onto webbing.

For parts that are tucked under other parts, such as the bird's tail feathers, make sure that you add a small seam allowance to tuck under. But in order to avoid a million tiny odd-shaped pieces, try also to cut as economically as possible. For instance, when cutting the cow, at right, cut the entire body outline, then appliqué the smaller pieces, such as the muzzle, on top. When outline is traced onto webbing, roughly cut out the shape, then lay cut-out piece, paper side up, onto the wrong side of a piece of fabric. Press in place with an iron, then cut out accurately around traced outline.

Remove backing paper (it will simply peel away) and iron motif onto background fabric, tucking pieces under others where applicable, before pressing. Machine-stitch around edges, using a close, narrow zigzag. Work decorative embroidery stitches by hand (see **Embroidery Stitch Guide** on page 112), as desired, using three strands of thread. Work eyes in French knots or satin stitch and nostrils in satin stitch.

Small Squares with Reverse Appliqué

Cut an 8cm square from double-sided webbing and trace chosen design onto centre of square. Apply webbing square to wrong side of fabric and cut accurately around edges of square. Cut out also the central design and any details, such as the windows of the house. Remove backing paper, then press and stitch the square to the background fabric, stitching both inner and outer raw edges. Finally, if applicable, press and stitch details in their correct place on the background fabric, within the cut-out shape. Using three strands of embroidery cotton, work a decorative border around edges of square, using photographs as a guide.

Basic Smocking Stitches

Cable Stitch

Bring needle up to left of pleat 1. With thread above needle, pick up pleat 2 in a small backstitch. This is an up cable. With thread below needle, pick up pleat 3 – down cable (**Step 1**). With thread above needle, pick up pleat 4 – up cable (**Step 2**). Continue with one up cable and one down cable across row (**Step 3**).

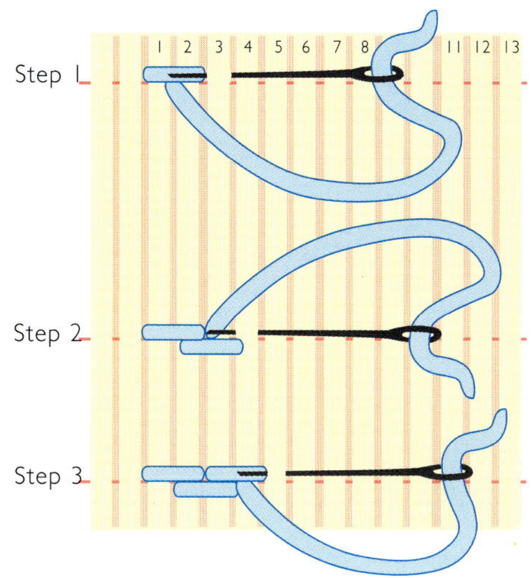

Graph for Angel Suit Sleeves and Pants

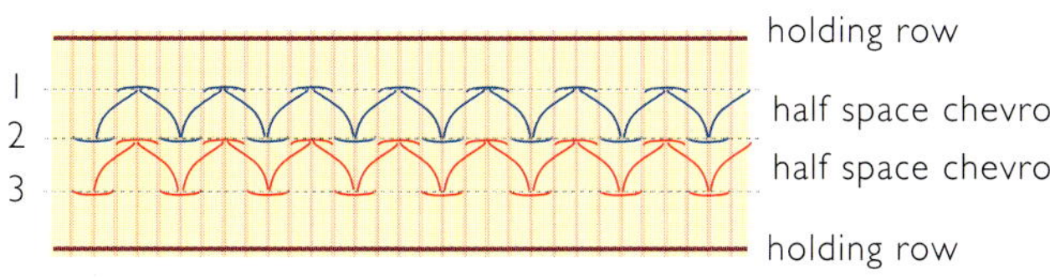

Graph for Angel Suit Yoke

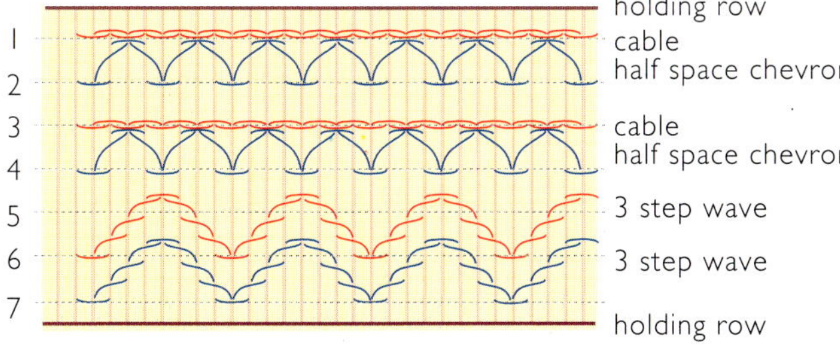

Full Space Three Step Wave Stitch

Bring needle up to left of pleat 1 on row B. Make a down cable through pleat 2 on row B. Keeping thread below needle, pick up pleats 3, 4 and 5, in turn, in the interval between rows A and B. With thread above needle, make an up cable through pleat 6 on row A. Keeping thread above needle, pick up pleats 7, 8 and 9 (to match pleats 3, 4 and 5). The next down cable picks up pleat 10 on row B. Continue across row.

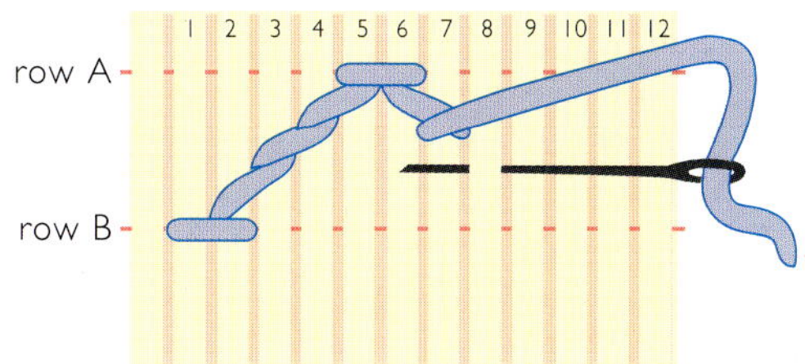

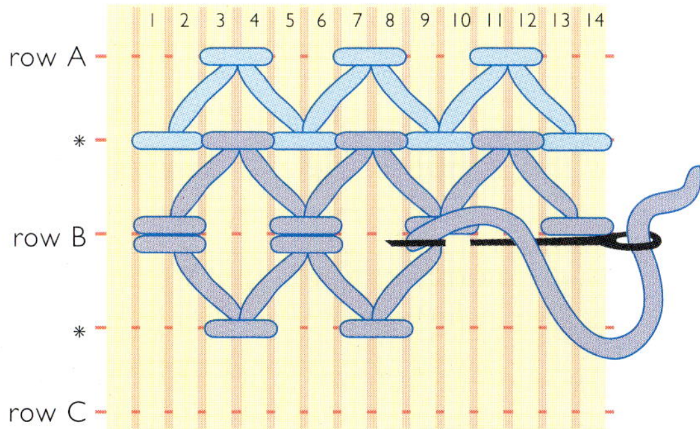

Half Space Chevron stitch

Bring needle up to left of pleat 1, halfway between row A and B, at point *. Make a down cable through pleat 2. Keeping thread below needle, pick up pleat 3, across interval between * and row A. With thread above needle, make an up cable through pleat 4. Keeping thread above needle, pick up pleat 5, to match pleat 3. Make a down cable through pleat 6. Repeat across row. Work second row exactly the same as first, beginning at pleat 1 on row B, thus creating a wave effect. Alternatively, the second row can be worked as a mirror image of the first, creating a diamond pattern.

Knitting and crochet notes

Tension

Correct tension is essential. If your tension is not exactly as specified in the pattern, your knitted item will be the wrong size. Before starting any pattern, make a tension swatch, at least 10cm square. If you have more stitches to 10cm in width than recommended, use larger needles or hook. If you have fewer stitches to 10cm than recommended, use smaller needles or hook.

Knitting abbreviations

alt: alternate; **beg:** begin/ning; **cm:** centimetre/s; **cont:** continue; **dec:** decrease, decreasing; **foll:** following; **garter st:** knit every row; **inc:** increase, increasing; **incl:** including, inclusive; **K:** knit; **0:** no rows, stitches or times; **patt:** pattern; **P:** purl; **psso:** pass slipped stitch over; **p2sso:** pass 2 sts over; **rem:** remain/s, remaining, remainder; **rep:** repeat; **rev st st:** reverse stocking stitch (purl all sts on right side of work, knit all sts on wrong side); **rnd/s:** round/s; **sl:** slip; **st/s:** stitch/es; **st st:** stocking st (knit row on right side, purl row on wrong side); **tbl:** through back of loop; **tog:** together; **ybk:** yarn back (take yarn back under needle from purling position to knitting position); **yft:** yarn front (bring yarn under needle from knitting position to purling position); **yfwd:** yarn forward (bring yarn under needle then over into knitting position again, thus making a stitch); **yrn:** yarn round needle (take yarn around needle into the purling position, thus making a stitch).

Knitting graphs

Work odd-numbered rows as right side and work even-numbered rows as wrong side unless it is otherwise stated.

Crochet abbreviations

alt: alternate; **approx:** approximately; **beg:** begin/ning; **ch:** chain; **cm:** centimetre/s; **cont:** continue; **crab st:** work as for dc, working from left to right, instead of from right to left; **dc:** double crochet; **dec:** decrease (insert hook into first dc, draw through and leave on hook, insert hook into next st, draw yarn through, yoh and draw through all 3 lps); **dtr:** double treble; **foll:** following; **htr:** half treble; **inc:** increase/s, increasing; **incl:** including or inclusive; **lp/s:** loop/s; **patt/s:** pattern/s; **rem:** remain/s, remaining or remainder; **rep:** repeat; **rnd/s:** round/s; **sl:** slip; **sl st:** slip stitch; **sp/s:** space/s; **st/s:** stitch/es; **tog:** together; **tr:** treble; **ttr:** triple treble; **yoh:** yarn over hook.

Table of British equivalents

Wool

8-ply = DK
10-ply = Aran
12-ply = Sport or Chunky
14-ply = Chunky

Knitting needles

UK size	Metric size (mm)
000	10
00	9
0	8
1	7.5
2	7
3	6.5
4	6
5	5.5
6	5
7	4.5
8	4
9	3.75
–	3.5
10	3.25
11	3
12	2.75
13	2.25